MW01124236

Answering God's Call

Reflections from the Lives of the Saints

by

Edward H. Trent

TELEMACHUS PRESS

ANSWERING GOD'S CALL

Cover designed by:
John W. Trent @ www.trentdesigninc.com
Telemachus Press, LLC

Cover art:
Copyright © Christimages.com

Published by Telemachus Press, LLC
http://www.telemachuspress.com

ISBN: 978-1-940745-36-7 (eBook)
ISBN: 978-1-940745-37-4 (paperback)

Version 2014.04.05

Printed in the United States of America

10 9 8 7 6 5 4 3 2 1

Have among yourselves the same attitude that is also yours in Christ Jesus,
Who, though he was in the form of God,
did not regard equality with God something to be grasped.
Rather, he emptied himself,
taking the form of a slave,
coming in human likeness;
and found human in appearance,
he humbled himself,
becoming obedient to death,
even death on a cross.
Because of this, God greatly exalted him
and bestowed on him the name
that is above every name,
that at the name of Jesus
every knee should bend,
of those in heaven and on earth and under the earth
and every tongue confess that
Jesus Christ is Lord
to the Glory of God the Father.

Philippians 2:5–11

In Loving Memory of Kay and Ed Trent
Who taught me and showed me what it meant to
Answer God's Call through a love only a
Mother and Father can give.

Answering God's Call

Reflections from the Lives of the Saints

Chapter 1

"BE STILL, BE Not Afraid." God told Elijah to be still and he would hear God's voice. God told David to be not afraid for God would protect him. These same comforting words apply to us as well. We must be still to hear God's voice in the quiet whispers of our hearts. We must not be afraid for the Lord is with us always to guide us and protect us. If, as we are called through our Baptism, we are truly to follow Jesus, we must be willing to pick up our cross and follow Him. We cannot be beholden to the things of this world, to things that keep us from doing the will of the Father. That is what we do as children of God; we follow Him wherever He may lead us.

But how do we do that and who can really teach us what it means to place Christ as first and central in our lives? There are too many different answers to the question, "What Would Jesus Do?" to give us much guidance. The question then is whether there are any real examples of what it means to do the will of God. Are there those who dared to "be perfect as [our] heavenly Father is perfect?" Are there examples of those who were like Christ in being "gentle and humble of heart?" Are there those who have loved others as Jesus has loved us?

The answer is yes, and there are lots of examples; we call them saints. Throughout my life, there have always been references to the saints. Christmas cannot be experienced without Mary and Saint Joseph. As a child, I was told that Santa Claus was just another name for Saint Nicholas, but I knew nothing of the real saint. Of course, I knew of the apostles, particularly Peter, James, and John. There were the authors of the Gospels,

Matthew, Mark, Luke, and John. I heard readings from the letters of Saint Paul almost every time I went to Mass. For Confirmation, I chose Saint Joseph as my patron saint. Still, I knew little of the lives they lived beyond what was written in the Scriptures and did not contemplate the fact that they were real people who started out not so different from me or anyone else.

Growing older, I learned of Saint Francis of Assisi. I knew Saint Augustine only became a saint because his mother, Saint Monica, prayed so hard for his soul. There were the heroes like Saint Joan of Arc. Attending Catholic school, I heard of Saint Elizabeth Ann Seton, but could not have told anyone anything other than she founded Catholic education in the United States. The saints remained people from long ago and their importance was not clear, other than they appeared on a medal or in a statue in church. There was always Saint Anthony who helped me find things that were lost and Saint Blaise who would protect me from ailments of the throat, so I never missed the blessing on his feast day, February 3. And then there was Saint Christopher who protected all travelers.

Narratives about the saints, however, are not merely stories from the past we tell children to encourage them to be good. Saints are not to be invoked as magic to help us deal with a particular issue, such as lost car keys. Saints are people just like us who lived their faith, who followed Jesus as He called them, who loved others as Jesus loved them. In short, saints lived up to their baptismal obligations. They are real life examples of people who made the conscious choice to pick up their crosses everyday and follow Jesus. They let us know that the promises Jesus made to his disciples are promises He keeps. Their lives remind us that when Jesus said He would always be with us, He meant it. The lives of the saints prove that with faith the size of a mustard seed, we can move mountains and transform the world.

Even so, the stories we hear of the saints are often daunting, leaving us with the belief that we could never be so faithful, so holy. There are the great theologians, the Doctors of the Church, who wrote about and explained great theological truths such as Saint Thomas Aquinas and Saint Teresa of Avila. There are the mystics who experienced the supernatural in their lives, and we certainly do not fit into their company. Given their incredible holiness, many are left wondering what studying the saints will do other than depress us by learning about what is likely not obtainable for us.

Saint Therese of Lisieux, who had an incredible childlike love of the Lord, felt the same way. She did not view herself as one who could produce great theological thought. She knew she was just a little child of God, unable to reach the heights of the great Church luminaries on her own. So, she would hold her arms open to the Lord and He would pick her up, taking her above the heights of even the greatest of saints. From there, she could experience the fullness of God's love and see all the wonders of God's creation. She knew that by doing simple, everyday things with a great love of Christ, we could all make a difference and bring glory to God. In doing so, we would become saints. So no one is incapable of becoming a saint, someone who lives for God; and by living for God, we live to share His love with all we meet.

My interest in learning more about the saints grew out of work I was doing in my home diocese to develop a plan for increasing vocations to the priesthood and religious life. In that work, the committee I chaired concluded that to develop more religious vocations, we needed to go back to basics, to who we are as Christians and as Catholics. Religious vocations are a part of who we are. Priests and sisters, like the saints, do not come down from on high, but come from local families. Priests first approach the altar from the pews, not walking out from the sacristy. They grew up with moms and dads, brothers and sisters, friends and neighbors who shaped their faith. They played ball or played with dolls, skinned their knees, and got into trouble, some more than others. We knew religious vocations were more often formed around the family dinner table than in the seminaries or convents. So, we needed to get families back to a strong Catholic tradition.

All of this got me thinking about what we could do to help families and parishes develop a culture of vocations. We all have heroes we look up to. These days, popular culture offers us athletes or movie stars or politicians, too often people who do more to denigrate a life of faith than promote one. But as Catholics and Christians, our life belongs to Christ. To walk with Christ, who better to emulate than the saints. But, if the saints were people we could never relate to, who were born with halos around their heads, then modeling our lives after them would be impossible. So it became important to know the saints as real people, to understand how they lived their lives and how they were called by God to the faithful service they rendered.

Throughout human history, God has given us examples to follow and voices to heed. First there were the prophets who constantly reminded the Chosen People of God's love for them and His commandments. In fulfillment of God's promise that began with Adam following The Fall, God sent His only Son into the world to offer the ultimate sacrifice of love. Jesus told us, "For God did not send his Son into the world to condemn the world, but that the world might be saved through him." (John 3:17) God wanted us to realize as never before how much He loves each one of us. He sent His Son into the world in the humblest of beginnings, being born of the Virgin in a stable hewn out of rock with his first visitors being shepherds.

During His life, Jesus taught His disciples and the people of His day of God's love. He called people to turn from sin—those things that separate us from God—and return to God the Father, our creator. Jesus distilled God's commandments into easy concepts to understand; we are to love God above all else, with our whole heart, mind, soul, and strength and love each other as He loved us. He laid down His life for us freely and without condition to show us the greatest love of all. Love is an easy concept to understand, but can be difficult to follow, something Jesus understood. This helps explain why He gave us the sacraments to feed and strengthen us with His grace and why He sent the Holy Spirit to guide us on this path.

Man's redemption comes from the Passion, Death, and Resurrection of Jesus Christ. This was the reason Jesus was born. He accepted the cup of crucifixion because it was the Father's will that, through the sacrifice of one, all may be freed from the slavery of sin and death. With His mission complete, Jesus entrusted the continuation of His work to the apostles. They were tasked with spreading the Good News of Salvation to all people. Throughout the history of the Church, saints have brought renewal to the Church and to her people. They were stark reminders of God's love and presence in our midst. They remind us of what we too often forget—that God is real, that He loves us, and that we are to follow Him. As God has always done, He chose the meek ones of the world to do great things, so there would be no doubt of who was responsible for the miracles in our world.

Saints were regular everyday people who had the courage and faith to say "yes" to God. They would be the first to tell you that they did nothing more than what God asked of them, which is what we are all called to do. If our faith is not evident from our actions, in how we live our lives, then our faith is not real. The saints remind us that if we "let go and let God," then God will do great things in our lives. They remind us that what Mother Teresa said was true, we are not called to be "successful," but to be faithful. By being faithful, we achieve the greatest success possible. They understood that being separated from God was the worst fate possible, so they lived in constant vigilance of trying to do the will of the Father in even the smallest and most insignificant of tasks.

In today's world, so many things vie for the hearts and minds of people. The aggressive social progressives and humanistic and materialistic philosophies all too present in today's society tell people that a life of faith, especially as expressed in the lives of priests and religious, is folly and empty. The message is that people like Mother Teresa are rare and only laudable because they help the poor, not because they serve selflessly out of a total devotion to God. A message we too often hear is that God may be a private matter for people, but God is not a message for nations and people in general. That message is as empty as a well gone dry and completely unable to quench the human desire for the Truth. Yet, as Christians, we know the Truth: Jesus is the Son of God, who was born of the Virgin Mary by the power of the Holy Spirit, who suffered and died for our sins, and rose again to destroy the power of death. We no longer live for ourselves, but for Him. That is what all the baptized are called to do, and what the saints did so faithfully.

This still does not answer the question of who are the saints—not who were they; for they live eternally with God as He promised. It also does not answer the question of how their lives are relevant in the 21st century. Yet, what I discovered in looking at the lives of the saints was that following Jesus in 30 A.D., 1300 A.D., or today is no different—it is all about following Jesus. We know He is the Alpha and the Omega, the same yesterday, today, and forever. His Truth does not change and His love is everlasting. The saints faced the same challenges we do today, even if most of them did so without having to compete with cable television or the internet.

The following chapters are reflections on the lives of just a few saints to draw attention to how they answered God's call to a religious vocation. Not everyone is called to a religious vocation, but we are all called to serve God as He calls us to serve Him. By studying the lives of the saints and learning from them, maybe we too will draw closer to the Lord and serve Him and our fellow man more faithfully. The transformation that comes from living our faith has the power to change the world. If it can happen for the saints and those they influenced, imagine what would happen if we all answered God's call in our lives.

These reflections come from talks I gave at my parish to help promote religious vocations. The theme came from Pope John Paul II's call to seminarians to Be Still … Be Not Afraid. We are to ask ourselves how Jesus is calling us. When we see the saints as people like us who got it right, we can honestly believe that in these days and in this time we too can answer God's call in our lives. In a lot of ways, we have it easier than the saints of centuries ago, but we all face the temptations of life and confront evil that is all too real in the world. Only by faith in the Author of Life and serving Him will it all make sense. Then we will truly experience what Jesus came to offer—that we might have life and have it abundantly. He does not give us more than we can handle. So, like the saints, we must trust Him completely, die to ourselves, pick up our cross, and follow Him. It matters not if we are a priest, plumber, painter, or politician; our lives belong first and foremost to Christ. We may suffer for our faith, but the rewards are worth the price, as you will see.

I have been blessed to hear from my fellow parishioners how much they enjoyed learning about the saints. There was almost always someone in the pews who had a special devotion to each saint we discussed. Several mothers told me how their small children looked forward to the talks on the saints and that they even started reading books on the lives of the saints at home. It became a challenge to see if they had read about the saint as I began telling the story. Our connection to the saints was obvious, they professed the same faith we profess.

Trying to be respectful of people's time when giving a reflection at the end of Mass, I attempted to limit my talks to no more than five to six minutes at first, but found the time growing to ten to twelve minutes to give even a mild amount of justice to the story we were to learn from the life of the saint. While I researched each saint as best I could for my purposes, I do not pretend to be an expert, a scholar, or a theologian. I am a regular guy who has been inspired by people who share my faith and lived it, so that at the end of their days they received the promise of heaven offered to everyone through Jesus Christ. I hope you find the lives of these saints as inspirational as I have and encourage you to learn more about a saint whose life resonates with you.

All of the saints share the most important things in common. They dedicated their life to the service of God. They picked up their crosses and followed Him. They endured suffering and ridicule by a world that did not understand why following Christ was the only thing that mattered in life; all else was superfluous. In the end, the saints experienced more joy, more peace, more love than anyone else during their lives because they went through life so deeply connected to Jesus. So, while you read these pages, Be Still ... Be Not Afraid, to What is Jesus Calling You?

Edward H. Trent

Chapter 2

MY REFLECTIONS ON the lives of the saints began as a way to create a culture of vocations in my parish. My pastor, Father Luke McLaughlin, wanted more than just a request that people pray for vocations, although prayer is very important. When I met with him and told him I wanted to do talks once a month, or so, on the life of a saint to discuss how the saint answered God's call in his or her life, rather than focus on the miraculous things that happened during the saint's life, he was willing to go along. I was certainly being ambitious in believing I could pull off what I had promised would be no more than five minutes on the life of a saint once a month while working and spending time with my family. First, the research required took more time than I imagined. Additionally, five minutes was hardly enough time to greet someone, let alone tell the vocational story of someone enrolled in the Book of Life.

Many parishes in the United States stick to a hard and fast rule of one hour for Mass; at least, many of the people in the pews believe there is or should be such a rule. My wife and I had been parishioners at our church for a number of years and knew some of the people there, but we were by no means household names. I was to give my reflections at all three Masses on the weekend. On those weekends, the Mass would go over the hour mark. I was uncertain how the purpose of the talks would be received and whether I could put together interesting talks consistent enough to keep people's attention. The last thing you want as you approach the altar to give a talk is to hear a loud groan from the congregation or watch people flee for the exits.

Father Luke and I decided an introduction the month before I was to start would be appropriate. He would introduce me and I would briefly explain what I was going to be doing. Given Father Luke's tenure at the parish, if he was going to let me give these talks, the people would put up with them for a while. If I did not do well, he would hear about it and my project would come to a quick end. To Father Luke's credit and my amazement, he never asked me what saint I was going to talk about and he never asked me what I was going to say. He heard each talk for the first time with the people in the pews. What follows are my introductory remarks on why we were going to explore the lives of the saints.

Introduction
(September 2006)

During my life, I have come to understand that we are participants in our faith, not simply observers. We know this from the teachings of Jesus and the teachings of the Church. We do not just remember events of long ago, but we share in and experience Jesus, alive and risen, today. Saint Paul tells us that by our Baptism, we are baptized into Jesus' death and resurrection. The life, death, and resurrection of Jesus are our reality, not just our memories or stories.

There are two sacraments that form the life blood of our faith, our daily encounter with Jesus in the Eucharist, and the Sacrament of Reconciliation. These sacraments are entrusted to the priestly ministry—to those men such as Father Luke, who dedicate themselves completely to God in service as a priest. Without the priest, we do not encounter Jesus in the Eucharist or His loving forgiveness in the Sacrament of Reconciliation. For us to be able to constantly have this encounter with Jesus, we must have priests—men willing to dedicate themselves wholly and completely to Jesus and the Church in this wonderful ministry, way of life, vocation.

Bishop [Victor] Galeone has asked that our diocese take the time to not only pray for an increase in vocations, but to take action to foster more vocations. For this to happen, it will take the prayer and dedication of each of us. The importance of such a commitment should be obvious. We have 52 priests in our diocese available for assignment to a parish and 50 parishes. I want to take a few minutes to tell you a little about what we hope to accomplish. Simply put, we hope to encourage more young men to become priests and more young women to become sisters.

Religious vocations come from us, the laity. We are called by our Baptism, by our invitation to the Lord's table, to "Be Still ... Be Not Afraid," to listen to Jesus and follow Him. Every priest and every sister started out just like us, with parents, brothers, sisters (lots of those in Father Luke's case), and each stepped forward from the pew to the altar.

Mothers and fathers do not lose their sons to the Church or their daughters to the convent. They have belonged to Jesus since their Baptism. Accordingly, we are asking you to help identify those who may have a calling to religious life by taking the time to notice and encourage those who impress you as someone who would make a good priest or sister. Tell them, "Hey, you know you'd make a great priest some day." It would be nice to say that out of this year's eighth grade class that we can add priest and sister to the long list of accomplishments when we remember them ten years from now. For that to happen, **we** must identify **our** future priests and sisters.

If you want to know what Jesus is calling you to do, then Be Still ... Be Not Afraid. So that is our theme, Be Still ... Be Not Afraid, to What is Jesus Calling You? As you approach the altar each week, ready to encounter Jesus, look at our youth a little differently and see a future priest or sister. Help them to Be Still ... Be Not Afraid. Jesus is calling them. Unless they are able to Be Still, they will not hear Him. Unless they are willing to Be Not Afraid, they will not be able to answer the call. Yet, that is what Jesus asks of each of us.

Each month we will hear someone's vocational story, a saint, Father Luke, even my own. We all have a vocational story. We will also present other programs and information that will hopefully inspire you to encourage our youth to consider a religious vocation. We all have a vocation in life, a calling in which we serve God. Given the number of priests we currently have with a growing Catholic population, more men are needed for this vital and wonderful vocation. To make that happen, it will take all of us. Who knows, one day we may have a priest who grew up at Saint Matthew's celebrate Mass here at this altar. With your help, there is no question that will become a reality.

* * *

With these words, my work was begun. People needed to be inspired to take a fresh look at their faith, their daily walk with Jesus. We walk as a community of faith, a Church, not as a single soul lost upon the sea. Scripture and the Sacraments would come alive in the lives of the saints. If we are all called to be saints, and we are, then we need to model our lives after other saints. To do so, we need to know more about the greatest of saints and there are many to choose from.

The saints we will look at here came from different walks of life, lived in every time period, faced varying challenges, and were often the most unlikely people to fulfill the unique and important role God had selected for them. What they each shared was an unshakeable faith in Christ, but that faith came to each at a time when God needed them to be about the business He had in store for them. Some came to faith late in life, others after questioning their faith, and others were born with a complete love of God. We walk with the saints because one of the saints walked the path we are called to walk. We may not all be a Saint Francis, but someone is called to follow the path he followed and set out for the Friars Minor. We all will not have visions of the Blessed Mother who tasks us with building a great cathedral while entrusting us with great secrets like Saint Bernadette, but other children and adults have been so blessed and entrusted with such visits and secrets, both before and since she lived. Some are called to be like Saint Therese who lived in total obscurity, but whose deep faith as expressed in the story of her life converted millions. There may be a future Pope John Paul II who grew up through the Nazi occupation of Poland to become one of the greatest popes in the history of the Church. Who knows? What we should never doubt is that we are called to follow Jesus, to share in His kingdom, and make His love visible in our lives. If there is something

God wants of us, He will make the impossible happen; we must only trust and follow Him.

I hope you enjoy this walk with the saints as much as I have. We have so many examples of people who have put faith into action to be perfect models of what we are called to be by our Baptism. As God worked in their lives, I pray He may work in yours and mine.

Chapter 3

OCTOBER 1ST IS the feast day of Saint Therese of Lisieux. Years ago, a friend recommended that I read her short autobiography *The Story of a Soul*. It was first published in 1899, two years after her death. In 1997, while chaperoning a group of high school students on a trip to Paris for World Youth Day, the group traveled to Alençon and Lisieux to visit places connected to the life of Saint Therese. During World Youth Day 1997, at the large outdoor vigil, Pope John Paul II declared Saint Therese a Doctor of the Church. She was not a lofty theologian, did not complete a high school education (though she was very bright and read many spiritual works), and was virtually unknown during her lifetime. Still, her story, published shortly after her death at the age of 24, instantly inspired millions of people. She synthesized the Gospel message so clearly and so beautifully that all could follow her "Little Way" and grow closer to Christ.

I had also read a book of letters between Therese and a young missionary priest that was the inspiration for my first talk on the life of a saint. Saint Therese wanted to be a missionary, but her health was never strong enough to allow her to live such a life. She was also committed to praying for the conversion of sinners and she was devoted to praying for priests. As a result, she was asked to correspond with the young missionary priest and serve as a spiritual sister. She used this opportunity to encourage this young man's vocation from afar and she had a dramatic impact on his faith. It was exactly the story I was looking for to set the tone for the series of talks I was to give. Given the amount of time I allocated for myself, about five minutes, there was not time to cover Saint Therese's life and the content of these beautifully written letters. This talk proved to be one of the shortest of all my talks and really left much out about the path Saint Therese walked. I will attempt to cure that here after setting out what I did say about this wonderful saint who is called The Little Flower.

SAINT THERESE OF LISIEUX
(October 2006)

With October 1ˢᵗ being the feast of Saint Therese, The Little Flower, I felt it appropriate that this month's vocations reflection be on the life of Saint Therese.

Her vocation story is not typical. She knew from a very early age that she wanted to enter the convent, even seeking permission from the Pope to enter at the age of 15 rather than 16. All four of her older sisters entered the convent, as well, three as Carmelite sisters like Therese later did.

Saint Therese is best known for her "Little Way." She realized that the key to faith is love, to be like God, who is Love. For such a young girl, this was not about doing great things, but doing the little, everyday things with great love and devotion to Jesus. This included sweeping the floor, washing dishes, obeying her superiors, all done with joy, great love, and out of service to Jesus. When my children are old enough, one of the first books they'll read is her autobiography, *The Story of a Soul*.

But what I want to focus on today is her devotion to pray for missionary priests. Therese wanted to be a missionary, but her poor health prohibited it. She struggled with her health her whole life, ultimately losing it to tuberculosis at the age of 24 on September 30, 1897. So Therese prayed for missionaries and priests and was ultimately asked to correspond with a young missionary who hoped to become a priest, Maurice Belliere.

In 1895, while in his second year of seminary, Maurice wrote to the Mother Superior of the Carmelite Convent in Lisieux, France, asking for a sister to pray for him. He was about to leave for a year of military service and feared that he would lose his vocation while out of the seminary. The

Mother Superior was Therese's older sister, Pauline, and she asked Therese to pray for and correspond with the young Maurice.

For the next two years, the two traded approximately ten letters each, during which Therese gave him comfort and encouragement. They talked about their vocations, with Therese giving great insight to the love of God. The following portions, taken from one such exchange, highlight the need for and power of Therese's prayers.

In a letter dated November 28, 1896, Maurice wrote:

My good little Sister:

The Lord is sending me a hard trial—as He does with those He loves—and I am very weak. Within a few days He will undoubtedly send me to the Seminary of the African Missions. My desire will at last be realized, but I still have to struggle with a lot. I have to break myself away from a number of cherished and strong attachments, as well as from some soft and expensive habits of easy living, from a whole pleasant and happy past which still strongly appeals to me. I need strength, my very dear Sister. Ask God to give me, with the clear light I need, the courage of a strong and noble self-surrender—as well as zeal for His glory, with the humility that is the foundation of holiness. The missionary has to be a saint, and a saint I am not.

In her December 26, 1896 response, Saint Therese wrote the following passages:

I assure you, Monsieur l'Abbe, that I am doing the very best I can to get you the graces you need. These graces will certainly be given you, because Our Lord never asks us for sacrifices that are beyond our strength. It is true that sometimes this divine Savior makes us taste all the bitterness of the chalice which He presents to our soul. When He asks the sacrifice of all that is most dear in this world it is impossible, apart from a very special grace, not to cry out as He did Himself in the Garden of His agony: "Father, let this chalice pass from me … nevertheless, not my will but Yours be done."

It is most consoling to remember that Jesus, the Strong God, experienced our weakness, that He trembled at the sight of His Own bitter chalice, the very one which He had once so ardently desired to drink.

Monsieur l'Abbe, your lot is truly beautiful, since Our Lord chose it for Himself and first put His own lips to the cup which He now holds up to yours.

* * *

Let us work together for the salvation of souls. We have only the only day of this life to save them and thus to give Our Lord some proof of our love. The tomorrow of this day will be eternity, when Jesus will reward you with the hundredfold of those sweet and lawful joys which you are giving up for Him. He recognizes the extent of your sacrifice. He knows that the suffering of those who are dear to you adds to your own suffering. But He too suffered this martyrdom. To save souls He too left His Mother; and He looked down at the Immaculate Virgin standing at the foot of the Cross, with a sword of sorrow piercing her heart.

She concludes: "Let us stay united in prayer and suffering, close to the crib of Jesus. Your unworthy little sister."

Maurice's next letter sounds like it is from a totally different person, someone strong in faith and confidence. We cannot underestimate the power of prayer and the importance of living a life grounded in the love of Christ.

So, pray for our priests and sisters and for those men and women being called to be priests and sisters that they may answer God's call, knowing that He will provide and care for them. You may not know their names, but offer up a prayer for all those called to religious life, so that in your Little Way, God's great love will be seen. As always, Be Still … Be Not Afraid, to What is Jesus Calling You?

* * *

As noted earlier, this does little to tell the story of Saint Therese and her story is remarkable. Canonized 28 years after her death, she quickly inspired generations. Her autobiography was written as an act of obedience at the request of her Mother Superior, who happened to also be her sister, Pauline, whom Therese loved very much. Her story in her own words has touched the hearts of millions. Her simple message of love is the sum and substance of the Gospel. Her vocation was love; to do everything she did with great love, whether it was greeting someone to sweeping the floor to suffering for the salvation of sinners. As we now know, she has indeed been permitted to spend her time in heaven showering roses on those who seek her help to follow Christ. This is her story.

Therese was born on January 21, 1873, in Alençon, France, the youngest of nine children born to Louis Martin and his wife Zelie Marie Guerin. They were loving and holy parents and both had considered a religious vocation before they married. Religious devotion was at the core of their family. Of their nine children, two boys and two girls died shortly after birth, leaving Therese the youngest of five surviving girls.

Therese was a precocious child. She feared doing wrong and became very upset when she failed to do good. She was also very stubborn. Therese's life was filled with joy when, at the age of four-and-a-half, her mother died. Her mother's death had a profound effect on Therese, leaving her very sad and drawing her closer and closer to her father. Her sisters and father all pitched in to care for the youngest in the family. With the death of her mother, Therese entered what she would call the second phase of her life.

Therese loved her father very much. She called him her "beloved king" and he would call her his "little queen." They often took walks in the garden and Therese would set up a tea party for her king. Her father was always attentive to his youngest and proved his devotion when she announced her vocation.

After the death of her mother, Therese looked to her oldest sister, Pauline, as her "second mother." She would go to Pauline for instruction and often confessed her transgressions to her. Therese was very devoted to Pauline, but her closest playmate was her sister Celine. They were practically inseparable.

When Therese was nine, Pauline entered the Carmelite order. Therese was again sad at the loss of her sister and mother and longed to join her as a nun. Therese was so distraught at the thought of losing Pauline that she fell gravely ill. Her father, sisters, and cousins prayed for her, but no medicine seemed to help. She suffered headaches, delirium, and constant fatigue. Her sisters and aunt kept a constant vigil with her. Then, two months into her illness, Therese had a vision. In her room was a statue of the Blessed Mother. On the Sunday of a novena being prayed for her recovery, Therese lay in bed when she called for Marie. Marie, Celine, and Leonie, knelt at her side and prayed to the Blessed Virgin for Therese. Therese then gazed at the statue, which shone with brilliance. As she gazed at the sight, Our Lady smiled at Therese. At once she was healed. Though no one saw the Virgin but Therese, Marie knew when her sister had been cured.

Therese turned toward Marie, another of her sisters, to fill the void left by Pauline's entry into religious life. Marie helped Therese prepare for her First Holy Communion. Therese desired, with all her heart, to receive Jesus in the Eucharist. To her delight, Therese received her First Communion on the same day Pauline took her vows at Mount Carmel. It was a day that drew her even closer to her older sister.

A few years later, Marie left for the convent. Therese could not bear to lose another sister and mother figure. She would cry often and craved affection. In time, Therese knew she had to grow up. A turning moment for her was at Christmas in 1886. In her autobiography, Therese describes her conversion that Christmas night in the following passage: "We went to midnight Mass where I had the joy of receiving almighty God. When we got home again, I was excited at the thought of my shoes standing, full of presents, in the fireplace. When we were small children, this old custom gave us such delight that Celine wanted to continue treating me like a baby as I was the youngest in the family. Daddy used to love to see my happiness and hear my cries of joy as I pulled out each surprise from the magic shoes, and the delight of my beloved King increased my own. But as Jesus wanted to free me from the faults of childhood, He also took away its innocent pleasures. He arranged matters so that Daddy was irritated at seeing my shoes in the fireplace and spoke about them in a way which hurt me very much: 'Thank goodness it's the last time we shall have this kind of thing!' I went upstairs to take off my hat. Celine knew how sensitive I was. She said: 'Therese, don't go downstairs again. Taking the presents out of your shoes will upset you too much.' But Therese was not the same girl. Jesus had changed her. I suppressed my tears, ran downstairs, and picked up my shoes. I pulled out my presents with an air of great cheerfulness. Daddy laughed and Celine thought she was dreaming! But it was no dream. Therese had got back for good the strength of soul, which she had lost when she was four-and-a-half. On this glorious night the third period of my life began. It has been the loveliest of them all and the one richest with heavenly graces."

Therese grew closer to Celine after that. She also learned the power and importance of prayer. In the paper one day, she read about a prisoner who was to be beheaded for murder. The article talked about his defiance, and Therese feared the loss of any soul, including this poor prisoner. So, she prayed for him, prayed that he would confess his sins and accept Jesus. She prayed, "I am sure You will forgive this wretched Pranzini. I shall believe You have done so even if he does not confess or give any other sign of repentance, for I have complete faith in the infinite mercy of Jesus. But I ask You for just one sign of his repentance to encourage me."

On the day after his execution, Therese looked at the newspaper and read that, as the prisoner mounted the scaffold he had still not confessed. Then, at the last minute, he turned and seized the crucifix offered to him by a priest, kissing the wounds of Christ three times. Therese had found her vocation, praying for the conversion of sinners.

Her desire to enter Mount Carmel only increased. Under the rules of the order, a girl had to be sixteen years old to enter the convent and Therese was only fourteen-and-a half. She told her father of her desire on Pentecost. Even with her young age, he could see the love she had for God and the love the Lord had for her. He gave his consent, but that was not enough. Therese ultimately got the consent of her uncle, but when she went to see Pauline, her sister told her that the Mother Superior said she would not allow Therese to enter until she was 21. Therese was devastated. Still, she had a champion in her father, so they made an appointment to see the local priest who was charged with overseeing the convent.

Her visit did not go well and she described him as cold and unyielding. Finally he told her that he was "only the Bishop's deputy. If he allows you to enter, I shall say nothing more." So, when her father offered to take her to the bishop, Therese quickly accepted.

Therese approached the appointment with much trepidation. As shy as Therese was, she had to overcome it and explain to the bishop why, at the young age of fourteen, she was prepared to enter Mount Carmel and dedicate her life to the Lord. The bishop was polite and kind, but he did not give his consent. In telling her father that Therese should stay at home a little while longer, her father showed his devotion to Therese's calling. He told the bishop with great deference that if the bishop did not give his consent, then while he was in Rome on the diocesan pilgrimage, they would speak with the Holy Father about Therese's desire to enter Carmel. The bishop was moved. While still not giving his consent, he told Therese that he would speak to the superior about her and that her trip to Rome would be a good one and it would strengthen her vocation. So, she left the Bishop's palace without a favorable reply to her request. She was to take her desire to Rome.

Three days later, she was off to Rome with her father and a group of pilgrims from her diocese. The priest who was part of her meeting with the bishop was also on the trip and he kept a close eye on her. Her trip would indeed strengthen her faith. She stood on the spot where martyrs shed their blood and gave their life for Christ. She was taken in by the history of the place, where so many men and women of faith before her had come, lived, prayed, and died, only to be reunited with the Lord in heaven.

On Sunday morning, November 20, 1887, the group went to the Vatican and celebrated Mass at eight o'clock in the morning, in the Chapel of the Sovereign Pontiff with Pope Leo XIII. The Gospel began with these words, "Do not be afraid, you, my little flock. Your Father has determined to give you His kingdom." The promise by Jesus to his apostles that they would share in His kingdom was what Therese longed to hear. The Gospel also recounted Christ's words to the apostles that He had to suffer before entering into His glory and that if the apostles wanted to enter, they too would have to drink from the chalice He was to drink. Therese was ready to do just that.

After Mass, she was able to have an audience with the Pope. The rules, as laid down from the bishop's assistant, were very clear; she was to walk up, kneel and kiss his ring, then rise and walk off. There was to be no talking to the Pope. Yet, when Therese knelt before the Pope, she looked at him with tears in her eyes and said, "Most Holy Father, I have a great favour to ask." Pope Leo leaned forward so that his face was right before hers. Therese then said, "Most Holy Father, to mark your jubilee, allow me to enter Carmel at fifteen."

The priest from her diocese, who was standing next to the Pope, responded that the local authorities were looking into the matter as Therese was seeking to enter Mount Carmel before the appropriate age. To this, the Pope responded, "Very well, my child, do whatever they say." Therese was not deterred and responded, "Oh most Holy Father, if you say yes, everybody will be only too willing." To this, the Pope responded, "Come, come … you will enter if God wills." With that, her visit ended.

Therese left in tears. She still did not have her answer. The remainder of her pilgrimage was amazing, but her thoughts and heart were on her plea to Pope Leo XIII. Therese viewed her relationship with Jesus in a very simple, childlike manner. She was his toy, a ball to be more precise. After her visit with the Pope, Therese said Jesus let His ball drop and then went to sleep, dreaming He was playing with the ball by bouncing it and letting it roll away before picking it up and holding it to His heart. There were times she felt abandoned in her quest to honor Him, but still always able to see Him, knowing He was there.

On January 1, 1888, she received word from the Mother Superior that on December 28, she received a letter from the bishop authorizing her immediate entry into Carmel. The Mother Superior went on, however, that she was going to make Therese wait until after Easter to enter. Therese was overjoyed and greatly pained at the same time. Her wish was granted, but she still had so long to wait. Therese entered Mount Carmel on April 9, 1888, when the Feast of the Annunciation was celebrated that year. As she entered, Therese announced her reason for coming, "I have come to save souls and above all, to pray for priests." This was to be her vocation.

Therese's life in Carmel was not an easy one. She was isolated and rarely saw her father. Many of the sisters thought she was too young and too immature to be in the convent. Still, she dealt with everything with joy, offering all of her sufferings to the Lord. On September 8, 1890, she took her final vows and was given her veil on September 24th. She took the name of Sister Therese of the Child Jesus and of the Holy Face.

One sister in particular was very hard on Therese. Still, Therese found herself often in this sister's presence. She assisted the sister in chores always keeping a cheery disposition. When the sister fell ill, it was Therese who took care of her. In the end, the sister became quite fond of Therese and Therese of her.

Therese lived by doing the little things in life with great love. Her health was not the best and she was often bedridden. Still, she sought no special treatment and always wanted to do what was asked of her. She knew she would never be a missionary, so she accepted her mission where she was, praying daily for sinners and for priests and growing closer to the heart of Jesus. Her love of Jesus was all consuming and she saw the incredible blessings the Lord shone upon her through revealing Himself to her in the quiet of her heart. She knew of His presence and of His love, so she shared that love with others. She knew she belonged to Jesus and there was nothing else in life that could bring such joy, such peace as knowing that the Lord held one close to His Sacred Heart. She took that knowledge and put it into everything she did. That was her Little Way.

Therese was soon put in charge of the novices. She was to teach them about religious life and their duties as brides of Christ. She did this cheerfully, but never growing too close to the novices. It was important for them to view her as a superior and not a peer. That does not mean she was cruel to them. Far from it. She taught them the love of Christ and how through their sufferings that could come in different forms they could bring honor to God and grow closer to Him.

In 1895, Therese was speaking with Marie and Pauline, the latter being prioress of the convent, about events from her childhood. Marie suggested to Pauline that Therese write the story of her childhood. Pauline agreed and made it an order; Therese, out of holy obedience, complied. So, in the quiet of her cell after a full day's work, Therese began writing. When finished with her childhood memories, Pauline felt the manuscript incomplete. But by then there was a new prioress, someone who would not understand the manuscript, so Pauline said nothing about it. When Therese fell ill once again, Pauline spoke up and asked that Therese be directed to complete her work as Pauline feared her little sister did not have long to live. The prioress agreed. In July 1897, Therese began the last two chapters of her story. Saint Therese died on September 30, 1897, at the age of 24.

Her manuscript was found and published locally with 2,000 copies in the original printing. It continued to sell steadily and *The Story of a Soul* has touched the life of everyone who has read it. Her story is one of love and a childlike relationship with Jesus. Life gets too complicated. We often miss the joy in the love of our Lord. Rather than see pain and disappointment in suffering, Saint Therese offered it up for the salvation of a sinner who had lost that connection to the Divine Savior. Her story reminds us of the everyday encounters with Christ. Too often, we miss Him in the mundane, but that is where we will find Him if our hearts truly belong to Him.

Saint Therese knew the importance of a holy priesthood. She prayed for priests constantly. Her words describe her devotion so clearly: "Another discovery I made concerned priests. Until then I hadn't been able to understand the main purpose of Carmel. I loved praying for sinners, but I was astounded at having to pray for priests. I thought their souls were without blemish. It was in Italy that I came to understand my vocation, and it wasn't too far to travel to learn that. I met many holy priests during the month I was away, but I saw that some of them were still men, weak and subject to human frailty, even though the sublime dignity of the priesthood raised them above the angels. Now, if prayers are needed for those holy priests whom Jesus called 'the salt of the earth,' how much more is it needed for priests of lukewarm virtue? For did not Jesus also ask: 'If salt loses its taste, what is there left to give taste to?' What a wonderful vocation we Carmelites have! It is up to us to preserve the salt of the earth. We offer our prayers and penance for God's apostles and we are their apostles, while, by word and deed, they bring the Gospel to our brethren."

With Saint Therese, we must pray for our priests. There are many good and holy priests and there are some who lack the strength to live out their vocation. All need our prayers, for they bring Christ truly present to all of us in the Gift of the Altar, the Eucharist. They administer the sacrament of Reconciliation for the forgiveness of our sins. They administer the

sacraments of Baptism and Confirmation that bring the gift of the Holy
Spirit to our souls. As Saint Therese prayed for young Maurice and all
priests, we must remember them in our prayers and pray that more young
men will follow their footsteps in serving Christ and His Church in this
holy ministry. They tread where the apostles tread. It requires an abandon-
ment of self and all we hold dear, but in doing so, they gain the promise of
heaven. Pray they learn to follow Saint Therese's Little Way to the Heart of
Jesus. For we should all desire our priests, who lead us in worship, to be as
close to the Lord as we hope one day to be and to share in His heavenly
kingdom.

Chapter 4

THERE ARE GREAT limitations in reviewing the life of a saint in ten minutes or less, but a reflection on some aspect of a saint's life is always beneficial. The life of a saint naturally draws one closer to the center of that life, which is the Lord Jesus. When it came to selecting a saint to discuss for my first Christmas talk there was never a question on who that would be, it had to be Mary, the Mother of God. She is the greatest example we have of living totally and completely for God.

THE BLESSED MOTHER
(December 2006)

It is hard to believe that the following words were uttered by a girl barely into her teens. "My soul proclaims the greatness of the Lord; my spirit rejoices in God my Savior. For he has looked upon his handmaid's lowliness." As she continues to do for us, Mary points to God the Father, acknowledging that all things are of His making and deserving of our praise. She leads all to her son so that we might see God.

Life for Mary was that of a typical girl in Nazareth under Roman rule. She was betrothed to Joseph, not by her choosing, but as set up by others. She most likely helped her mother with the cooking and cleaning around the house. One night as she prepared to sleep, the Angel Gabriel appeared to her with the news that she was chosen by God to bear a Son. While we

consider children a gift from God, and that they are, for Mary, this pregnancy before she was married meant death under the law. But when the
Angel told her of God's plan for her, Mary did not hesitate, but said, "Let it
be done to me according to thy word."

Of course, Mary did not sit around waiting to see what would happen
or how people would react. She immediately set off to care for her cousin,
Elizabeth, who was in her old age, but for the first time, pregnant. Rather
than think of herself, Mary, still the new teenager, set off on a journey to
assist another in the birth of a child, a boy to be known as John the Baptist.

The mysteries of these early years were only beginning. Mary was faced
with Joseph's understandable disbelief at her revelation that she was pregnant, not by some other man, but by God. She could only trust that God's
plan for her would be fulfilled. Of course, when Joseph chose to stand by
her, Caesar Augustus's decree sent her on a long journey just as her pregnancy was to come to an end. She found no room in the inn, but rather a
patch of hay in a stable, most likely on the hillside.

We all know the story of that first Christmas night. Shepherds arrived
to see the child and told of angels singing. A few days later, when present-
ing Jesus in the temple, Simeon spoke in wonder of the child and told Mary
of the great suffering she would experience as Jesus grew older. Anna, the
old woman in the temple, also spoke of the child. Then there were the three
men from the East bearing gifts, speaking of a king. We know from Luke's
Gospel that Mary pondered all these things in her heart. She was still a
young girl, giving birth to a son as foretold to her by an angel, but so many
people seemed to know more about her son than she did.

Without being able to get comfortable, Mary and Joseph were warned
to flee, not home to Nazareth and their family, but to Egypt because Herod
sought to kill the child. So, it was first in Egypt and then, after the long
journey back home to Nazareth, that Mary watched her son grow up. This
little boy, who played with the other children, got dirty by playing in the
mud, and skinned his knees when he fell, would grow up to challenge
everything that everyone knew about God and the promised Messiah, and it
was her responsibility to teach him of God's love and plan for him. In the
end, Mary would watch Jesus suffer and die upon a cross like a common
criminal.

It is easy to think that with the Angel Gabriel's message, Mary was fully aware of what was taking place in her life. But the angel never told her just who the child was, only that she would bear a son, name him Jesus, and he would sit on the thrown of King David. There was no discussion that this child to be born was God Himself. Even with all that happened in those early years, up until the time Jesus was hanging upon the cross, Mary had to proceed on faith that she was following God's plan for her life.

We come to know God through Mary and her willingness to say yes to God's call. We are called, as Jesus tells us and Mary shows us, to hear the Word of God and do it. In Mary we see, firsthand, that God asks us to participate in our own salvation. Jesus could have appeared on the scene from out of nowhere, but instead chose to be born of this young girl and grow up just like every small boy of the time. For salvation to be possible, we, like Mary, must trust that God will do the impossible. We must be willing to say "yes" to His plan for our lives and follow Him knowing it will lead to the cross, but also to the resurrection. God offers us great things; indeed, He offers us His only Son. We only have to be willing to say "yes."

Additionally, as with Mary, we must have faith that God will give us all we need to walk the path he sets before us. When the Angel appeared to Mary, he declared that she was "full of Grace" and that "the Lord is with thee." Indeed He was, as we see in our readings over the Advent and Christmas seasons. Even when Jesus was hanging on the cross about to die, He was not going to leave Mary alone, but entrusted her to the care of Saint John. Jesus is always there for us and gives us our families, each other, the Church, to help us as we walk the path God asks of us in our life.

We must be willing to follow it and encourage others to follow the path God has for them. During Advent and throughout the year, spend some time in prayer and reflection on what God is asking of you. Spend time with your children and ask them what God may be asking of them. The first step is being open to whatever God may be calling them to, even if that means a call to the priesthood or religious life. The greatest gift we can present to the Baby Jesus at Christmas and all year long is ourselves. So, Be Still … Be Not Afraid, to what is Jesus calling you?

* * *

Some question why Catholics have such devotion to Mary. The reason is simple; the Lord Himself was and is greatly devoted to her. She is the greatest example of holiness we have. From the Cross, Jesus gave Mary to all of us as our mother and she intercedes for us before the Father. We walk where she walked, which includes the journey to Bethlehem, the exile in Egypt, the return to Nazareth, and ultimately the path that leads to the foot of the Cross. Saint Therese cried when she saw a picture of Christ Crucified with no one in the picture to catch His precious blood being spilled for the salvation of all, yet Mary was there when all others ran away. Mary was there in the upper room on Pentecost and received the gift of the Holy Spirit. It is easy to imagine the comfort and grace she gave to the apostles as they began their mission of spreading the Gospel. She is there for us as well.

Another classic reason for Catholics to be so devoted to Mary is because Jesus could refuse her nothing. The story of the wedding feast at Cana, where Jesus performed his first public miracle, describes this so well. The bridegroom ran out of wine, a great embarrassment on the happiest day of his life and that of his new bride. We do not know why, as the predicament was surely not known publicly as of yet, but the issue came to Mary's attention. She took the head waiter to Jesus. Mary simply presented the problem to Jesus. "They have run out of wine." When Jesus looked at her quizzically and said, "What concern of this is mine?" Mary must have smiled as she ignored the comment and turned to the head waiter. She told the head waiter what she tells each of us, "Do whatever He tells you." With that, she walked away and Jesus was left with nothing to do but answer her prayer on behalf of the bridegroom. Jesus did just that, but not in a small way. Rather, in answering Mary's request on behalf of the bridegroom, He not only turned water into wine, He turned water into the best wine and lots of it. That is what God does for us when He answers our prayers.

Mary continually takes her children to Jesus. Her life consisted of drawing people's attention to her Son who gives life to all. She reminds us that God will touch our lives in ways we could never imagine. She continually tells us "Do whatever He tells you." It is no wonder that the Hail Mary is a prayer you hear on the lips of every Catholic. We sing the praises of the Angel and of Elizabeth when we say, "Hail Mary, full of grace, the Lord is with you. Blessed art thou among women and blessed is the fruit of your womb, Jesus." Our prayer that follows is simple, "Holy Mary, Mother of God, pray for us sinners, now and at the hour of our death." We have but two important moments in life, the now in which we live and the hour of our death when we will meet God face to face. It is during these times we want Mary there to intercede for us, to present our needs to the Lord and ask Him to fill us with His mercy and grace. If He can fill water jugs with the choicest of wines, imagine what He can do with us.

Chapter 5

MARY'S REACTION TO being called by God was one of humble submission. For another, his reaction could not have been more different. We have the benefit of 2,000 years of testimony regarding Jesus, but His disciples had to make their decision to follow Him truly on blind faith. They may have had the benefit of hearing His voice, watching Him interact with others, witnessing the miracles, but their eyes and ears could also deceive them. Some follow quietly, others follow kicking and screaming, and others cannot help bumping into their own ego or preconceived notions. For Peter, God had great plans for him and saw within him all of the abilities and qualities God would mold to allow Peter to accomplish all God had in store for him. Peter was hesitant at first but learned to trust in God and became the head of the Church, an exalted position that carries with it the weight of the Cross.

SAINT PETER
(January 2007)

My sister-in-law includes a saying at the end of all of her emails, "God doesn't call the equipped, He equips the called." When we look at the saints, we have a tendency to forget that they were born and grew up just like us, regular, everyday people. Those are the kinds of people God calls to do His work, common, everyday people. Indeed, that is just what Jesus did when He called Saint Peter.

Peter was born in Bethsaida on Lake Genesareth. He ultimately settled in Capharnaum, another town on the lake, and became a fisherman. As the owner of his own boat, he made a good living. He was married, with his mother-in-law living in his house.

Peter was an ordinary man of the time. He was humble, but hot-headed. He often said whatever was on his mind. He professed bravery, but ran away at the first sign of trouble. Yet, this is the man upon whom Jesus chose to build the Church.

When the Lord first called him, Peter was returning from a long and unsuccessful day of fishing. Jesus sent him back out to try again. Rolling his eyes and at the exhortation of his brother, Peter did as Jesus said and caught so many fish his nets almost tore in two. When he arrived back on shore, Peter fell at Jesus' feet and said, "Depart from me, Lord, for I am a sinful man." Still, Jesus asked Peter to follow Him and He would make him "a fisher of men." So, Peter did, leaving behind a successful business to follow Jesus.

As rough around the edges as Peter may have been, Jesus saw three important qualities He could nurture so that Peter, of all men, could stand at the head of the new Church. Jesus saw that Peter was a man of deep faith, he was fiercely loyal, and he was a natural leader.

Peter often stepped up when the other disciples were not quite sure what to say. This was Peter, the one who would speak whatever was on his mind, not worrying about what others were thinking. When Jesus asked the disciples "Who do you say that I am?" Peter spoke up and said, "You are the Christ, the Son of God, the one who was to come into the world." Later, after Jesus told the people that "He is the Bread of Life" and "His flesh is real food," many left and would no longer follow Him. Jesus asked the disciples, who were themselves questioning his teaching, if they too were going to leave Him. Immediately, Peter spoke up saying, "To whom shall we go. You have the words of everlasting life. We have come to believe that you are the Holy one of God."

Of course, Peter sometimes put his foot in his mouth. When Jesus told the disciples that he must suffer and die, Peter rebuked him and said he would forbid it. In response, Jesus had to put him in his place. The same thing happened at the Last Supper when the Lord was going to wash his feet, Peter refused, believing it beneath Jesus to wash his feet. When Jesus told him that such a refusal would mean Peter would have no part of him, Peter said, "Then not only my feet, but my hands and head as well." We, of course, remember Peter's denial of the Lord three times before the cock crowed. But, earlier that night, as Jesus was being arrested in the Garden, Peter drew a sword and cut off the right ear of the High Priest's slave, only to again be rebuked by Jesus.

To mold him, Jesus included Peter in some very special experiences. Peter was present when Jesus raised a young girl from the dead, and he was also present during the Transfiguration. He was permitted to see who Jesus really was, so that no matter how many times he fell in life, he would get back up and continue to follow Christ.

After Jesus' Ascension, Peter became the voice of the Church. Immediately following Pentecost, Peter stood on the balcony and told people from all over the world that Jesus who had been crucified had been raised from the dead. When called before the Sanhedrin, Peter did not run in fear as before, but boldly proclaimed Jesus as Lord. People flocked to him, even placing the sick on the side of the road, hoping his shadow would fall upon them and they would be healed. This, the same temperamental fisherman who denied even knowing Jesus in his darkest hour, was now the unmistakable leader of the new Church.

For him to spread the Gospel to the ends of the earth, Peter had to accept that God was calling Gentiles to know and follow Jesus, as well. Even though it was against Jewish law, Peter entered the house of Cornelius, a centurion, and after telling him of Jesus, baptized him and his family. Peter also stepped up to recognize that the Lord had called the great persecutor of the early Christians, Paul, to be a great disciple. Peter's acceptance of Paul following Paul's conversion was critical to the Church spreading throughout the Roman Empire. Without question, Peter's leadership was instrumental to the Church's rising influence in the early years after Jesus returned to heaven.

Peter's faith led him all the way to Rome, where he was crucified upside down, not believing himself worthy to die as Jesus did. This fulfilled the only hint Jesus gave him of times to come when Peter was charged with feeding and tending His sheep. Jesus told him that a day would come when men would bind him and take him where he did not want to go. And so it was. Peter also kept his hasty promise to Jesus at the Last Supper, that he would die for Him.

Peter did not know where he would be going when Jesus asked him to follow Him. There was no way for him to comprehend all he would see in his journey through life, but he followed anyway. Peter lived the faith he professed, not because he had what it took, but because Jesus selected him and he said "Yes." God then gave Peter all he needed to fulfill the plan He had for him in his life, and it was a great plan. All this because Peter trusted what Jesus said to him and was willing to follow Him wherever the Lord was going to take him.

The same is true for us. We do not get to see any farther down the road than today. We must believe that He will give us all we need to walk the path He sets before us, knowing and trusting that He will walk each step of the way with us. We must be willing to trust that when Jesus calls us He is not making a mistake. None of us are born "equipped" to fulfill a ministry as a priest or sister, but those willing to answer that call will find that God will equip them with all they need. All we must do is trust and follow Him. So, Be Still … Be Not Afraid, To What is Jesus Calling You?

* * *

There is a lot we can learn from Saint Peter. First, none of us is perfect. We are going to make mistakes; we are going to put our foot in our mouth. We each have our own personalities and God will use them to His purpose if we are willing to let go of our pride. It took Peter a little while to learn that lesson even though there is no doubt Peter loved the Lord so very much. We have to be humble enough to ask for forgiveness and accept forgiveness for our sins. We have to be willing to get up and start marching forward once again. We have to be humble enough to say, "Yes, Lord" when He calls us and then set out to do what we have been called to do.

Even though, at first, Peter ran when there were signs of real trouble, when it was his time to step up, Peter did just what the Lord needed of him.

Peter boldly professed Christ resurrected in the face of imprisonment and ridicule from the people he only recently feared. Jesus told Peter that he was "the rock upon which I will build my Church" for a reason, and it was Peter's faith, as revealed to him by God the Father, that proved to be that reason. Peter had to learn to live the faith he professed and to do so bravely. In the end, he did just that.

We cannot help but respect Peter's profession of faith and his courage following the resurrection. With Peter, Jesus established something that will not end, His Church. Within His Church, Christ placed the fullness of God's truth and sent the Holy Spirit to guide her. With Peter, in communion with the other apostles and disciples, the Church contains the fullness of the Gospel message. It is through the Church that we receive God's grace when we receive the sacraments, those outward signs established by God that give us life in Christ Jesus.

Peter was Christ's vicar on earth as the visible head of the Church following Christ's ascension into heaven. After Pentecost, the faithful looked to him and he relied on those who walked the same road of faith he did. When Peter spoke on behalf of the Church, he did so, filled with the Holy Spirit. So, too, do Peter's successors, when speaking in the name of the Church on matters of faith and morals. Not all of them may have been worthy of the title, but the sins of popes, priests, or people do not dilute the truth of Christ's teaching as found in Scripture and Sacred Tradition. It is this Truth that forms the whole of the Church's teaching for this Truth is Christ Himself. Jesus promised He would be with the Church until the end of time, and He has, protecting her from error even in light of the personal failings of each of us.

There may be a time when someone will ask you to walk away from Christ or from His Church due to the sins of a follower of Christ. If so, how will you answer? Should you be asked, remember Peter's response when Jesus asked the disciples if they, too, wanted to leave Him, "Master, where shall we go? We are convinced you have the words of everlasting life." Like Peter, let us follow Jesus always, living in the fullness of His truth that comes down to us from the apostles.

Chapter 6

MARTYRDOM IS NOT limited to the early Church. Peter may have been crucified upside down and Steven may have been stoned to death, but the secular world killing Christians did not stop with the conversion of Rome. The essential element for the martyr is 'for whom is he laying down his life?' Few are faced with the choice of laying down their lives for their faith and fewer still are actually called upon to "lay down his life for his friends." When it happens, we should take notice. That sacrifice does not come about on the spur of the moment, but due to a faith that has been nurtured to the point of maturity. So it was with Saint Maximilian Kolbe.

SAINT MAXIMILIAN KOLBE
(February 2007)

The night before he died, Jesus told his disciples, "Greater love no man has than this, to lay down his life for his friends." Is it really possible for someone in this day and age to take these words literally, to step into the shoes of a friend and accept death so the other might live? Well, Saint Maximilian Kolbe did just that. But as remarkable as the way he died, even more remarkable is the way he lived, in total trust in God and the Blessed Virgin Mary.

Born on January 8, 1894, Raymond Kolbe grew up in Russian-controlled Poland. He was the second of five boys, but two of his younger brothers died before the age of four. Raymond's parents were weavers, living in one room of a house where other families occupied the other rooms.

Raymond was known as a wild child, always running around with lots of energy and getting into mischief. His mother tried first to straighten him out with a switch, but the whippings did little to curb his enthusiasm. Then at the age of 12, Raymond made a sudden change for the better. Once again caught in mischief, his mother whipped him good, but for the last time. While praying and crying before the statue of the Blessed Mother they had in their home, Raymond had a vision of Mary. He had prayed to her asking what would become of him, a question his mother often asked. In response, Mary appeared and showed him two crowns, a white one meant he would persevere in purity and a red one meant he would become a martyr. When asked which one he wanted, Raymond said, "I'll take both."

The family did not have enough money for school, but a group of Franciscans from the Austrian zone of Poland came to town and offered to school any of the boys in the area who would commit to becoming friars. Raymond and his older brother immediately signed up.

At age 16, Raymond had a decision to make, either continue on, forgoing marriage and family forever, or leave the seminary. He told his older brother that he did not think the religious life was for him because he liked math and science too much and wanted to be an inventor or join the military. As they went to tell the Father Superior, they were stopped in the hallway and told they had a visitor. Their mother had come. She had news that their younger brother was going to follow them in becoming priests. Raymond did not have the heart to tell his mother he did not want to continue, so he remained and entered the novitiate, taking the name of Maximilian Maria.

Maximilian was ultimately sent to study in Rome. He excelled in school, obtaining his doctorate and was ordained on April 28, 1918. While there, Maximilian, who had a great devotion to the Blessed Mother, started the Militia or Knights of the Immaculate with a small group of friends. Their purpose was the conversion of souls and the growth of holiness, all under the protection of Mary.

Returning to Poland, Maximilian understood the influence of modern technology and sought to use it to spread the word of God's love. He asked for permission to begin a newspaper, *The Knight of the Immaculate*. He did not have any money or a place to house a printing press, but trusted that Mary would intercede for him. She did. The paper started and circulation quickly grew to over 5,000 copies each month and the number of people joining the Franciscan Order to assist with the work was remarkable. Soon, Father Kolbe had outgrown the monastery where he was and needed new space.

Again, he trusted in Mary's intercession. When told the cost of the land, Father Kolbe knew he had no way to pay for it. So, he put a statue of Mary in the field he wanted and prayed for her help. When driving by the land one day, the owner saw the statue and decided to gift the land to Father Kolbe. Along with a handful of other friars, Father Kolbe built housing and a printing press. Within ten years, there was a seminary, missionary training, a fire station, a radio station, and a population of more than 700 Franciscans. *The Knight* had grown to a circulation of 750,000, not to mention the other publications being written and printed on site. The monastery was its own city, with a name meaning "Marytown, the City of the Immaculate." In addition, during all of this, Father Kolbe also started a monastery and newspaper in Japan, even though he could not speak the language and was given no money for his venture.

On September 1, 1939, the Nazis invaded Poland. The Germans were suspicious of Father Kolbe because he spoke the truth of their oppression and ethnic cleansing. On September 19, 1939, the Gestapo showed up on his doorstep. Father Kolbe was arrested for writing articles against Hitler and sent to a prison camp just across the German boarder. On December 8th, the feast of the Immaculate Conception, he was released.

Returning to his City of Mary, Father Kolbe found ways to serve the three thousand refugees left for him. He rebuilt the city and kept people's spirits up. He even managed to get permission to publish one issue of *The Knight*. Then on February 17, 1941, the Germans again arrested him. This time, he was sent to Auschwitz and became prisoner number 16670.

The rations were minimal, a cup of coffee in the morning and weak soup and half a loaf of bread after work. Yet, Father Kolbe would share his rations when someone else needed them more. Even though praying was forbidden, Father Kolbe would kneel at his bed at night and pray. He would also offer comfort to those around him, praying with them and offering words to lift their spirits. The labor was extremely hard. Starved, beaten and at least once attacked by a dog, Father Kolbe was barely able to keep up with the work assigned to him, which was often worse when the guards learned he was a Catholic priest.

To keep prisoners from escaping, not only were there guards who would shoot at the first sight of flight, dogs, and harsh conditions, but if one member of a group escaped, then ten would be starved until the prisoner was caught. No one ever survived from that group of ten.

One day, a member of Father Kolbe's barracks of 200 men escaped. The others were forced to stand at attention all day without any food or water while the guards looked for the prisoner. Not finding him, the head guard began picking ten men who would be placed in a starvation cell. After five or six were chosen, the next man was selected. He began to cry, explaining he had a wife and two sons. The guards did not care, but Father Kolbe stepped forward and requested that he be exchanged for the other prisoner. Although shocked by the request, it was granted. Father Kolbe and nine others were placed in a starvation cell on July 31, 1941. On August 14, four of them were still alive, including Father Kolbe, despite having no food or water. Because the cell was needed for other prisoners, these four were injected with carbolic acid. As the doctor bent down to him, Father Kolbe held out his arm and smiled. His body was removed the next day, the Feast of the Assumption. One of the guards explained later that he often heard singing and hymns coming from the cell when Father Kolbe was there or witnessed him kneeling with the others, talking to them.

The prisoner who was spared by Father Kolbe's heroic act survived the war and was reunited with his wife, but his two sons had been killed when their town was bombed in the war. He, along with others who managed to survive the atrocities of the Nazis, spread the word of Father Kolbe's sacrifice. It was another son of Poland, Pope John Paul II, who canonized Saint Maximilian Kolbe on October 10, 1982.

Father Kolbe's belief that God would provide and that Mary would intercede for him was steadfast. He was the model of charity. He did not just preach turn the other cheek, but he did so, until his death. Saint Maximilian Kolbe's life, even more than his death, is the true example of being a disciple of Jesus, serving others and preaching the truth, no matter the consequences. He accomplished his goals in life, he converted souls, he helped others grow in holiness, and he became a saint.

We have a duty to follow Jesus no matter where he leads us. Father Kolbe dreamed big, always focusing on God. He simply followed the path God inspired him to follow, and did so, not for his own glory, but for God's. With his final steps, Saint Maximilian Kolbe showed how great he loved by sacrificing himself for another. Are you ready to follow in his footsteps, the same steps Jesus asks us to follow? Be Still ... Be Not Afraid, To What is Jesus Calling You?

* * *

Saint Maximilian Kolbe is a wonderful example of perseverance in one's vocation. Saint Kolbe took on a daunting task in trying to reach as many as possible through the printed word. He had no idea how to make it happen, but through prayer and dedication, he accomplished what seemed improbable. But he did not stop with his published papers, which helped spread the faith to so many; he even went to a foreign land halfway around the world to open a monastery in Japan. He did so when travel was not easy, and he did so in a land that was to be as much at the heart of World War II as the invading Germans.

Saint Kolbe established a monastery that sat on a hill overlooking Hiroshima. The Christian faith did not dominate Japan as it did Europe, but with the coming war, the presence of the monks would prove to be a powerful reminder of God's love to those living there. This would be especially true following the outcome of the war and the manner in which it ended. While Saint Kolbe only helped to get the monastery started, he planted seeds of faith in a part of the world that desperately needed to hear the Gospel.

There were many obstacles to Saint Kolbe's mission, but he continued to persevere and God allowed his work to flourish. When it came time for him to face what could only cause one's blood to run cold, his arrest and imprisonment in a concentration camp, Saint Kolbe did not lose hope and was not deterred from doing God's work. When he was released nearly three months later, Saint Kolbe returned to his monastery and continued his work, even though his work is what got him arrested in the first place. He was challenged with the needs of so many who made their way to his door, but he worked to keep everyone's spirits high. His life was to share the love of Christ, even in the midst of Europe's darkest hour. He did so, even though he risked another arrest, an eventuality that occurred in early 1941.

In a world of utter despair, Saint Kolbe knew his vocation was to share God's love with those he met. Those sent to Auschwitz were sent there to die after being subjected to the cruelest treatment. Even here, Saint Kolbe relied on his faith and God carried him through. Saint Kolbe found a way to bring joy and hope to people in a place that was designed to strip people of anything good. When Saint Kolbe was sent to Auschwitz, God went with him, as He did with so many of those subjected to those horrors. When a man was selected to die because another chose to run for freedom, Saint Kolbe did not hesitate, but stepped up and offered himself in the other man's place. His sacrifice was rewarded with joy at his death and the other man surviving to be reunited with his wife.

Jesus offered Himself as the sacrifice to bring salvation to the world. Jesus offered Himself for the forgiveness of sins. We are all called to sacrifice all we have, including our very life, to bring about God's kingdom. Saint Kolbe did just that, a sacrifice that left a lasting impression on everyone in the devil's den that was Auschwitz. While walking in the shadow of death, Saint Kolbe did not fear any evil for Jesus was at his side. Jesus will walk with us, as well, we just need that same kind of faith.

Chapter 7

DURING LENT, I felt it appropriate to take a look back at the five saints we had discussed in the preceding months. The saints we had discussed could not be more different from each other while sharing the same unshakable faith. God worked differently in the lives of each, while each accepted the path God set before him or her. In looking at this group of saints together, it became evident that each of us just needs to focus on how God works in our life, on our vocation and not on what someone else is doing. We take comfort from the lives of saints and seek to emulate their faith, even though we may not be called to live our faith in the same way. There is only one Blessed Mother and only one Saint Peter. Not everyone is called to start a newspaper, a hospital, or other major undertaking. What we are called to do is to grow closer to our God and listen to what He has in store for us. Then, we must follow Him.

LENT 2007

As we travel through Lent and prepare for Easter, some of us may think about how we are going to make it if we give up chocolate, alcohol, or some other indulgence. In August 2006, we, as a parish, undertook to consider, pray for, and promote religious vocations. During this time, we have reflected on the lives of five saints, five people who were willing to be still and be not afraid and to say yes when God called them to live a life of service for Him. Lent is a good time to reflect on how their sacrifices not only mirror those of Jesus, but were made possible because of Jesus' passion, death, and resurrection. It is an appropriate time to stop for a moment and reflect on how, although living in different circumstances and some living 2,000 years apart, their stories all have a familiar theme.

Saint Therese knew she wanted to be a Carmelite nun from an early age. She followed several of her sisters to the convent. She did nothing we might call heroic, except love so deeply that her simple story has inspired millions and earned her the title of Doctor of the Church with such great theologians as Saint Augustine and Saint Catherine of Sienna. In a very simple way, she exemplifies what we are all called to do, love; love God above all else, love our neighbor, pray for those who stray and do evil. In doing so, she took the time to write to a young seminarian who was studying to be a priest and a missionary. Saint Therese's words of love and support, and no doubt her fervent prayer, carried the young Maurice through his journey to becoming a priest. She realized that the life of the Church and the lives of all who believe depend so much on having good, holy priests. She saw a priest even in the distraught letters of a young, extremely ordinary man she had never met. We should take the time to see such potential in the young people around us, even those at our dinner tables, in our schools, sitting now in our pews, or even the faces we see in the mirror and encourage them to be still and be not afraid so they can hear God's call and follow it.

Saint Padre Pio's life sounds as if it must have occurred during the time of Jesus or certainly around the time of Saint Francis, in the 1200s, and not one that did not end until 1968. His life is a reminder that God will do the extraordinary in our lives if we are willing to let Him. Sometimes, the extraordinary includes extraordinary suffering or the ability to bring about extraordinary change in the lives of the people we meet. From the story of his life, I was struck by the actual, physical wounds matching the wounds Christ received on the cross, the same cross we venerate on Good Friday. Then, I was struck that the reason for those wounds was for the forgiveness of our sins. The fact that Saint Padre Pio was an amazing confessor, one that people would wait in line for days just so he could hear their confessions, is no longer surprising to me. What was surprising is that so many who did stand in line were people not active in the Church and would never have thought of entering the confessional, yet they sought him out for that very purpose. The power of the sacrament, the incredible power to hear the words of absolution and know your sins, no matter how great or how small, are forgiven, is overwhelming. As we approach Easter, the feast that brought about our salvation from sin, I realize how much we need priests to administer the sacrament of reconciliation.

Of course, we are all guided by the example of the first and greatest of all the disciples and saints, the Blessed Mother. It was helpful to remember she was just a young, certainly frightened, teenager that first Christmas. Yet, when God asked the impossible of her, she said yes. Then, when the world went dark on that Good Friday, she remained by her Son at the foot of the cross. Those two images, as different as they are, say the same thing, we are to follow Jesus wherever He leads us. She did that. I also know that we can count on her to intercede for us, just as she did at the wedding at Cana. We will receive the answer to our request if we, like the servants there, "do whatever He tells us." God called her to her special place in salvation history when she was only a teenager, the time we should definitely be encouraging our children to think about how they will answer God's call, even if He leads them into religious life as a priest or sister.

While Saint Therese, Saint Padre Pio, and the Blessed Mother were obvious saints from the time of their childhood, Saint Peter was not. He was rousted out of a comfortable fishing business in his adult life to drop everything and follow Jesus. He literally followed Him across the known world before accepting the cross of crucifixion in Rome. While we must encourage our young people, we should not forget our young adults, even those with careers, as the Lord may be calling them too, and asking that they drop everything and follow Him into religious life. Their worldly experience would be invaluable to them in service to the Church as a priest or sister. I realize from the life of Saint Peter that God may call you to incredible things at any time, even when you think things are finally settled.

Another child unlikely to become a saint was Saint Maximilian Kolbe, who had only became a priest because he did not have the heart to tell his mother he wanted to do something else with his life. Yet, what he did as a priest is remarkable. Before emulating Christ's love by laying down his life for a complete stranger, Saint Maximilian Kolbe realized that modern technology, in his day newspapers and radio, provided excellent tools to spread the love of Jesus and explain the Church's teachings to others. This poor Polish boy's creativity and ability to do things beyond his wildest imagination were not limited when he became a priest, but expanded. Through his newspaper, he showed hundreds of thousands of people he would never meet what following Jesus meant. He helped others realize that Jesus is the Way, the Truth, and the Life. He taught people to dismiss the propaganda of the Nazis in his day, or, in ours, portions of popular culture. He let me know that to change the world, you cannot sit on the sidelines. We have to be willing to follow Jesus and trust Him, even if that means a last minute change in plans to accept a calling to be a priest or sister.

Lent is a time to prepare for the glory of Easter by remembering and experiencing the suffering of Jesus' passion and death upon the cross. We experience the fullness of Easter because so many men and women before us chose to follow Jesus in service as a priest or sister. Each generation must have those who will step forward to continue building the kingdom of God in service to the Church in religious life. That responsibility now falls to us and our children. We must come to realize that a vocation to religious life is not a life of suffering and want, but rather a wonderful way to celebrate and live the joy of Easter every day. Saint Therese did. Saint Padre Pio did. Saint Maximilian Kolbe did. We can, too. So Be Still … Be Not Afraid, To What Is Jesus Calling You?

* * *

Lent is a time of self-denial, a time to go into the wilderness, a time of preparation. As we prepare for Easter and meditate on Christ's life, death, and resurrection, do we consider how we are called to share in Jesus' passion, death, and resurrection? How do we prepare for life's greatest challenges? How do we prepare to meet Jesus face to face? Do we, when ridiculed for our faith, remain steadfast, knowing it is more important to follow God than man like Saint Peter did when called before the Sanhedrin following Pentecost? Do we handle adversity, criticism, and doubts about us with love as Saint Therese did and Saint Padre Pio did? Do we face daunting challenges with faith as Saint Maximilian Kolbe did, knowing that if it is God's will, then He will protect us and welcome us into heaven at a time He chooses? Can we, upon hearing God's voice, but not knowing "how this can be," respond with the fullness and humility of Mary?

Easter is a very, very powerful time and the most holy celebration of the year. It is the fulfillment of Jesus' life and God's promise to Adam, Abraham, David, and us for the redemption of souls and the forgiveness of sins. It is a time when all Christians walk the road to Calvary and witness again the life freely given. We cannot begin to imagine the depth of God's love for us, but we are called to live a life of faith, trusting in that love no matter the circumstances. It was that faith that allowed the saints to follow Jesus as they did in this life and to receive the promise of heaven when their time on Earth was done. God offers us the greatest gift there is, life with Him in heaven for all eternity. My prayer for myself, my family, and all people is that we will not hesitate to accept God's love and share all that it means to be His disciple, His saint.

It became very obvious early in my study of the saints that there is no mold for what the life of a saint would look like. For certain, the life of a saint is not lacking in life experiences or an understanding of the human condition. Saints are not people locked away in prayer without a clue as to the pressures and temptations of everyday life. Quite the opposite. The saints knew exactly what the people around them were experiencing, their challenges, their hopes, their fears. The saints themselves faced the same challenges and had hopes and fears of their own. What set them apart is that they were willing to follow Jesus all the way to the end, knowing as Peter proclaimed to Jesus, "We have come to believe that you are the Christ, the Son of the Living God." The Lord invites all of us to walk with Him. The question is whether we have the courage to do so.

Chapter 8

EVEN AS THE world and our culture changes, it is important to re-member that heroic lives of faith are not only possible, but they are all around us. In spite of what we read in the headlines, some will show a depth of faith we thought only possible in storybooks or that was to be found only in Scripture. In our time, God selected a girl born in a small town in Albania to share His love in a very remarkable way with those soci-ety forgot, or wanted to forget. Mother Teresa chose to live among the poorest of the poor to share with them God's love, because all people are made in the image and likeness of God. Mother Teresa lived her life to minister to those who found themselves excluded from and shunned by society. God needed someone to walk the path she followed, and while Mother Teresa set out on that path alone, she would always have the Church's support, and soon, she would be joined by people from around the world who helped her share God's love with the poorest of the poor.

BLESSED MOTHER TERESA
(April 2007)

The King said, "I was hungry and you fed me, thirsty and you gave me a drink; I was a stranger and you received me in your homes, naked and you clothed me; I was sick and you took care of me, in prison and you visited me." The people asked when they did these things and the King answered,

"I tell you, whenever you did this for one of the least important of these followers of mine, you did it for me." The point of Jesus' parable was to teach us to see the face of Jesus in EVERYONE we meet, even the outcast, the unwanted, the abandoned; to not just look upon those it pains us to see, but to do so with such love that we see Jesus in them. A young Albanian girl did so and changed the world.

Mother Teresa of Calcutta was born Agnes Gonxha Bojaxhiu on August 26, 1910, in Skopje, Albania. Her father was a successful merchant and member of the town council, but died in 1919. Her mother was left to care for Agnes and her two older siblings, sister Aga and brother Lazar. Although there was money on her mother's side of the family, she had no way to claim it, so times were not always easy for them. Still, her mother had a special place in her heart and at the family dinner table for the poor. She instructed her children, "Welcome them warmly, with love. My child, never eat a single mouthful unless you are sharing it with others." Once a week, Agnes's mother would visit an old woman abandoned by her six children and take her food, clean her house, and bathe the alcoholic woman covered with sores.

The family was fiercely Catholic. Agnes was active in her youth group, led by a priest who often shared stories from the missions, usually from India. Although considered rather "ordinary" and an average student, Agnes declared her desire to enter religious life and serve as a missionary. At first, her mother refused consent, but ultimately relented, telling her she must be "only, all for God and Jesus." She took that instruction to heart.

At the age of 18, Agnes headed to Rathfarnham, Dublin, Ireland with a friend from home to enter the Sisters of Our Lady of Loreto and spend six weeks learning English. From there, after taking the name Sister Mary Teresa of the Child Jesus, after Saint Therese of Lisieux, they set sail for India, a trip that took well over a month. Upon arriving in Calcutta, she spent the next two years in spiritual study and preparing to be a teacher. She had to learn Hindi and Bengali, while still perfecting her English. On May 24, 1931, after taking her temporary vows, she began teaching in the Loreto convent school in Darjeeling.

Even in these early days, the young Sister Teresa was exposed to the poor. One incident in particular surely helped form what would later

become her "call within the call" to work with the poorest of the poor. A
man arrived at the convent with a bundle from which protruded what the
young sister thought were two dry twigs. They turned out to be the emaci-
ated legs of a boy so weak that he was on the verge of death. Mother Teresa
recounted the incident as follows: "The man is afraid we will not take the
child, and said, 'If you do not want him, I will throw him into the grass. The
jackals will not turn up their noses at him.' My heart freezes. The poor
child! Weak, and blind—totally blind. With much pity and love I take the
little one into my arms, and fold him in my apron. The child has found a
second mother."

On May 24, 1937, Sister Teresa professed her final vows of poverty,
chastity, and obedience, earning the title of "Mother." She continued to
teach and also served as principal at the school in Calcutta until September
1946. It was then, when directed to go on retreat in Darjeeling due to her
health, that on the 10th of the month, she received her call to leave the convent and work and live among the poor of India.

While on retreat, she focused on the words Jesus spoke on the Cross,
"I thirst" and discussed her desire with her spiritual director. Although she
was determined, it was not as if she could just walk out the front door and
do what she wanted. She had submitted to the service of God and obedience to her order and the Church. To test her conviction, the local
Archbishop, who had to approve her request before she could submit it to
the Vatican, made her pray about it for an entire year.

In January 1948, the Archbishop finally gave his approval for her to
make the necessary requests to leave the convent and work with the poor.
Word came from Rome on April 12, 1948, granting her request. On August
16, she traded her habit for the sari she became so famous for.

Still, before Mother Teresa could head out to work among the poorest
of the poor, the Archbishop required her to obtain some medical training.
In December 1948, Mother Teresa stepped out into Motijil slum. She
quickly started a school for children living there; there were two rooms, one
for teaching academics and one for teaching basic hygiene. She had to overcome natural suspicion of her actions, especially being a foreigner and a
Catholic working among Hindus and Muslims. She found a one room
apartment to live in, one large enough for her to have a small chapel and

house the first of the women to join the new congregation. The first of the new sisters arrived on March 19, 1949, a former pupil of Mother Teresa's. A second joined a month later. In addition to their work and state of poverty, Mother Teresa insisted on time for prayer, attending Mass and spiritual reading. To serve Jesus in the poorest of the poor, the Sisters needed to be close to Jesus and strong in faith.

Starting a new congregation was not a simple process. Mother Teresa worked on the Rules of the Order and on October 7, 1950, the Feast of the Most Holy Rosary, The Sisters of the Missionaries of Charity was officially recognized. Her first home was for the dying. Those rejected and left on the side of the road needed to die knowing they were loved and to do so "beautifully" as Mother Teresa described it. Many were beyond hope of recovery, but none were beyond the love Jesus had to offer them through the compassion of the Sisters. Whenever the Sisters needed anything, God provided it when they needed it, whether it was food, money, medicines, volunteers, or property. Their mother house, the one they still use today, was gifted to them by a Muslim moving to Pakistan in 1953. Homes for the dying, clinics for lepers, schools and homes for abandoned children, and places for people to get a bite to eat were all begun with prayer and devotion to their purpose.

In 1965, at the request of Pope Paul VI and the Archbishop in Venezuela, Mother Teresa opened her first home outside of India, in Cocorote, Venezuela. Her work, blessed as it was by God, continued to spread. The Missionaries of Charity grew beyond anyone's wildest imagination. She received awards and acclaims from all over the globe, including the 1979 Nobel Peace Prize and some of the highest civil honors from the United States and the Soviet Union. She started homes and branches of the Missionaries of Charity in over 50 countries, opening her 565th convent in 1996, with over 4,000 sisters, not to mention brothers and volunteers. Mother Teresa died on September 5, 1997.

Mother Teresa knew that her work was dependent on Jesus, which made the presence of a priest everywhere she went essential. During a talk she gave to the Congress on the Family in France in 1986, Mother Teresa explained the importance of priests to her work. "Several years ago, the president of Yemen asked me to allow some Sisters to go to that country.

He wanted a home of the Missionaries of Charity to be established in Yemen. That country had been deprived of Catholic priests and nuns for six hundred years. There were no tabernacles there, no churches, no parishes! It was a completely Muslim country. I told the president, 'I am willing to allow the Sisters to go if you give permission for a priest to go with us. Because without Jesus, we will not go.' And then the president gave us permission. I had never before realized the greatness of the priesthood until I saw it in Yemen. When the priest came, the altar, the tabernacle, and Jesus came with him. All those years there had not been an altar, a tabernacle, or Jesus. Now we have three houses there, with three tabernacles in them. The people that come to work there use our homes as centers of prayer. This is the greatness of the priesthood!"

Mother Teresa looked at everyone by not seeing their weaknesses, their brokenness, their disease, but the face of Jesus inside of them. All human life, created in the image and likeness of God, was and is sacred. The poorest of the poor, the outcast, those others walk by, abandoned, were not only welcomed, but loved with a love Mother Teresa had for Jesus Himself, because, whatever she did for the least of his people, she did it for Him. Are we willing to see Jesus in those around us? For such faith, as it was for Mother Teresa, we must have Jesus. For Him to be present in the Church, we must have priests. So Be Still ... Be Not Afraid, To What is Jesus Calling You?

* * *

Mother Teresa was an untiring voice for good. She modeled what Saint Francis called his followers to, that is, to "spread the Gospel always, and if necessary, use words." Mother Teresa's example and tireless effort inspired thousands who left the comfort of home to live among and help the poorest of the poor. She spoke the truth always, even if the audience was not receptive to her message. She saw the intrinsic value of every human life, from its beginning at the moment of conception to its ending when God called His child home. She chastised presidents, prime ministers, cultures who failed to see the beauty of all life, who missed the face of Jesus in the child, the outcast, the invalid, the dying. If we will not see what lies beneath, what is at the core of our existence, we miss the beauty of God's creation. Mother Teresa did not miss it at all.

A film crew went to Calcutta to film Mother Teresa at work and document her mission. It was hard for them to understand how speaking so sweetly to someone in such pain, to wash someone who had not bathed in months or years, who was about to die, made any difference. After a time, they came to understand that we all deserve to be treated with dignity, even if it is just before we die. Mother Teresa had no way of curing everyone who came to her door, at least not physically, but she could touch their heart and soul by sharing with them the love God has for them. When they got home, they noticed in the developed film a soft light filling the rooms where Mother Teresa and her sisters worked. There were no lights in the rooms and there was no explanation for the illumination they saw. They concluded that the light could only be the visible love that Mother Teresa and her Daughters of Charity shared with the people God brought to their door.

A humble girl from Albania took the message of God and His infinite love to the ends of the Earth, including the corners kept in darkness for centuries because she answered God's call and He took over from there. Imagine what He can do for us if we have just a little of that faith. Mother Teresa's life is another example of what God can do with us if we just trust Him. He has a plan and when He calls on us to take on a role in this life, we need to be ready to say "Yes" no matter what the request. Amazing things will happen if we do.

Chapter 9

IN 1993, POPE John Paul II traveled to Denver, Colorado for World Youth Day. A large group of high school students from Jacksonville, Florida made the trip. The preparations took a year with lots of fundraisers to earn the money. The city of Denver had to prepare for nearly a million young people from all over the world arriving to celebrate, pray, and worship with the Pope. I was fortunate to get one of the few tickets our diocese received for the Papal Welcome in Mile High Stadium. Our seats were about 30 rows from the field and the Pope drove by in the Popemobile as he entered the stadium. The crowd had been waiting on his arrival and cheering at every step as it was shown on the giant stadium screen. When the Pope entered the stadium, the crowd went wild. The event was incredible, with more energy in one place than I had ever experienced or have experienced since. Watching the Pope greet people from around the world struck me deeply. His touch of a cheek, with tears in his eyes, was very moving. It showed how much he truly loved and cared for the young people around the world. Pope John Paul II, at that moment, personified everything I could imagine the Vicar of Christ being.

Later, at the vigil in Cherry Creek Park, with a million young people camping out under the stars for the closing Mass, there were several incidents that left a lasting impression on me and many of those present that night. One in particular was a young man with Down's syndrome who spoke about his journey of faith. He talked about working so hard to get a place where he could live on his own, getting a job, going to church. He concluded, "Holy Father, I came here to tell you, 'I love God.'" The crowd erupted and the Pope was deeply moved by his testimony.

Finally, the next morning, the Pope sat down after giving his homily during the Mass. He spoke about the importance of living the Gospel. In doing so, he spoke about the challenges young people face when trying to live a life following Jesus. He told the young people to stand up for the Truth and to not be afraid of the Gospel. Yet, when he sat down, he paused for a few moments and then said, "The Pope, he misspoke. He misspoke when I said, 'Don't be afraid of the Gospel.' No, be proud of the Gospel." The crowd went wild. Pope John Paul II lived a life that was proud of the Gospel, a life that let everyone know that following Jesus brought life and brought it abundantly. No wonder the theme for World Youth Day 1993 was John 10:10 "I came that you might have life and have it to the full."

The love so many people, young and old, had for Pope John Paul II was incredible. That same awe and excitement was evident for World Youth Day 1997 in Paris. Again, over a million young people gathered to pray and worship with the Pope and they were so excited. Paris was never more alive than when Catholics of good will from all over the world gathered to celebrate their faith with the Successor of Saint Peter.

Pope John Paul II did more than stir up a crowd as if he were a rock star. He got an entire generation of Catholics excited about their faith by sharing faith in Jesus Christ as it was meant to be shared. He stood up, proud of the Gospel, and preached the Truth. When he did, people followed.

BLESSED POPE JOHN PAUL II
(May 2007)

Just before He ascended into heaven, Jesus told the disciples that they would be His witnesses in Jerusalem, throughout Judea and Samaria, and to the ends of the earth. For one man, he would literally take the love of Christ to Jerusalem and the ends of the earth. Karol Wojtyla, who came of age under German occupation of Poland and later under Stalinist communism, would become the 263rd successor of Saint Peter and take the messages of hope, redemption, peace, freedom, and dignity to people in all parts of the globe. The subtleties of the workings of the Holy Spirit that led him to his vocation in a world that sought to deny God's very existence and exterminate those who most represented faith in Christ, is at the heart of his remarkable story.

Karol Wojtyla was born May 18, 1920, in Wadowice, Poland. His mother died when he was nine-years old, and his older brother, who had become a doctor, died when Karol was 12. This left Karol with his father. After completing high school, Karol and his father moved to Krakow. Karol had graduated as the valedictorian of his class, was an accomplished actor, loved literature, and enjoyed the outdoors, especially hiking, skiing, and canoeing. Being a priest was not in his plans.

His father died of a heart attack on February 18, 1941, three months before his 21st birthday. Years later, Karol discussed the effect his father had on his vocation, which at the time of his father's death was still 18 months away. "I was left alone with my father, a deeply religious man. Day after day I was able to observe the austere way in which he lived. By profession he was a soldier and, after my mother's death, his life became one of constant prayer. Sometimes I would wake up during the night and find my father on his knees, just as I would always see him kneeling in the parish church. We never spoke about a vocation to the priesthood, but his example was in a way my first seminary, a kind of domestic seminary."

Karol had just completed his first year of university, when on September 1, 1939, the Germans invaded Poland. Resistance was swiftly conquered. Although the fall term began as scheduled, it was not to last. On November 6, 1939, the Nazis called the faculty together, and 184 of their number were arrested and shipped off to the concentration camps where many would perish. So, the next year, Karol began four years of labor in the Solvay chemical plant, often walking 30 minutes each way to work. It was on one of these walks, in February 1944, that Karol was hit by a German truck and left for dead on the side of the road. A woman on a trolley saw him and was able to get help to get him to the hospital, where he spent several weeks recovering.

Academics were not the only ones to suffer under Nazi rule, which had as its goal to remove Poland and Polish culture from the map. Three thousand six hundred forty-six Polish priests were arrested and sent to the concentration camps, where 2,647 died. Indeed, from Karol's home parish in Debniki, most of the Salesian priests were arrested and sent to the concentration camps, where one was executed for refusing to grind rosary beads into the ground with his foot.

The tight grip of the Nazis had its effect on everyone. The entire country lived in fear. People were shot in the streets for failing to stop when ordered, or for not having their papers. Others were rounded up and their names posted on lists of those executed. Karol lost many friends to the Nazi brutality, including one of his fellow seminarians who was arrested one night by the Gestapo. The young man's name appeared on the execution list the next day.

The effects of the war on Karol's vocation to the priesthood cannot be understated. He described it this way, "All I can say is that the tragedy of the war had its effect on my gradual choice of a vocation. It helped me to understand in a new way the value and importance of a vocation. In the face of the spread of evil and the atrocities of the war, the meaning of the priesthood and its mission in the world became much clearer to me."

Indeed, it must have, for when Karol began his seminary training in the fall of 1942, he had to do so clandestinely under the direction of the Archbishop; the Nazis had shut down all of the seminaries. Such an act could bring about his execution and the execution of those who taught him. He had to keep up a double life, working and finding time to study. In 1944, Karol stopped going to work after the Nazi crackdown in August of that year. He escaped notice by the Nazis because his foreman was kind enough to remove his name from the roll of employees so he would not appear missing.

When the Nazis were driven out by the Soviets in 1945, many hoped things would return to normal, but they did not. Out of the darkness of Nazism and communism, Karol developed a profound understanding of and concern for the dignity of every human person and the need to respect human rights, beginning with the right to life.

On November 1, 1946, in the Cardinal's chapel, Karol Wojtyla was ordained a priest. Fifteen days later, he would make his first trip outside his homeland to study in Rome. Returning to Poland, his priestly ministry focused on young people and families. When traveling with them on their yearly canoeing and hiking trip, he asked to be called Wujek, or Uncle, so that the Communists would not cause them trouble. Indeed, a car had to be sent to him during one such trip in 1958 to bring him back to Krakow because he had been named an auxiliary bishop by Pope Pius XII. He was 38 years old. Five years later, he would become the Archbishop of Krakow.

As a bishop, Karol participated greatly in the Second Vatican Council, often addressing issues of religious freedom, the problems of modern atheism, and an increased role for the laity. In 1967, at the age of 47, Karol was made a Cardinal by Pope Paul VI. During all this time, Bishop, then Archbishop, and ultimately Cardinal Wojtyla would press the Communist government on religious freedoms and celebrate Mass before crowds that made the government very uncomfortable.

Then, on October 16, 1978, Cardinal Karol Wojtyla was elected the 263rd successor to Saint Peter, taking the name of John Paul II. He traveled the world as pope, including preaching to over one million in his native Poland in 1979, an event that marked the beginning of the end to communist rule. He was probably seen in person by more people than anyone who has ever lived. He continued to stress the dignity of the human person, and the inherent nature of our connection to God. As pope, he never lost touch with what people in all walks of life experience everyday and how it is critical for them to know, love, and worship God. He died on April 2, 2005, and the beatification process has already begun. [Pope John Paul II was declared Blessed on May 1, 2011, and will be canonized on April 27, 2014.]

The nature of his vocation can be seen in a comment he made to the crowd gathered for the closing Mass of World Youth Day 1993, in Denver, Colorado. During his homily he spoke to the young people about being counter-cultural, to stand up for what is right. They were to be the leaders. He told them to not be afraid of the Gospel. He told them he loved them and that the Church was counting on them.

After sitting down and a few moments of silence had passed, he spoke again. "The pope misspoke when I said 'do not be afraid of the Gospel.' No, be PROUD of the Gospel." The crowd let out a delirious cheer.

Are we proud of the Gospel, of the love Jesus has for us, each one of us? Are we willing to reject those things that degrade and undermine the dignity of the human person? Are we willing to see the value of the priest-hood in making Christ present, really present to everyone who approaches this altar? The priest is a necessary and indelible sign of our times and of all time, for Jesus calls men such as a young boy from occupied Poland to follow the steps of Saint Peter, and young men from Saint Matthew's parish to follow his example and serve as a priest. Be Still ... Be Not Afraid, To What is Jesus Calling You?

* * *

The impact of Pope John Paul II on our generation cannot be overstated. He revitalized the Church in so many areas. He sought out to atone for the sins of those who acted in the name of the Church. He showed humility but also stood firm when it came to doing what is right. He lived the example of what it means to be proud of the Gospel. His writings, his words, his presence let you know that God is real, that God loves you, and we have a choice to make in life. For Pope John Paul II, the only choice was to pick up his cross and follow Jesus. The story of the Pope's life and the impact he has had on so many cannot begin to be covered in these few pages. His harrowing escape from the Nazis, his challenges to Communism, his influence on a country and then the world are astounding. Now, our job is to take that same youthful exuberance and put it into our daily lives. That excitement for Jesus should pour out of us at it did from him.

Pope John Paul II's motto was Totus Tuus. As Pope Benedict XVI explained during his homily at the beatification mass for his predecessor:

Dear brothers and sisters,

Today our eyes behold, in the full spiritual light of the risen Christ, the beloved and revered figure of John Paul II. Today his name is added to the host of those whom he proclaimed saints and blesseds during the almost twenty-seven years of his pontificate, thereby forcefully emphasizing the universal vocation to the heights of the Christian life, to holiness, taught by the Conciliar Constitution on the Church *Lumen Gentium*. All of us, as members

of the people of God—bishops, priests, deacons, laity, men and
women religious—are making our pilgrim way to the heavenly
homeland where the Virgin Mary has preceded us, associated as
she was in a unique and perfect way to the mystery of Christ and
the Church. Karol Wojtyla took part in the Second Vatican
Council, first as an auxiliary Bishop and then as Archbishop of
Kraków. He was fully aware that the Council's decision to devote
the last chapter of its Constitution on the Church to Mary meant
that the Mother of the Redeemer is held up as an image and
model of holiness for every Christian and for the entire Church.
This was the theological vision which Blessed John Paul II discovered as a young man and subsequently maintained and deep-
ened throughout his life. A vision which is expressed in the
scriptural image of the crucified Christ with Mary, his Mother, at
his side. This icon from the Gospel of John (19:25-27) was taken
up in the Episcopal and later the papal coat-of-arms of Karol
Wojtyla: a golden cross with the letter "M" on the lower right and
the motto *Totus tuus,* drawn from the well-known words of Saint
Louis Marie Grignion de Montfort in which Karol Wojtyla found
a guiding light for his life: *Totus tuus ego sum et omnia mea tua sunt.
Accipio te in mea omnia. Praebe mihi cor tuum, Maria*—"I belong entirely to you, and all that I have is yours. I take you for my all. O
Mary, give me your heart" (*Treatise on True Devotion to the Blessed
Virgin,* 266).

As God entered the world through the consent and womb of Mary, so
we, through the guidance and intercession of the Blessed Mother, experience and come to know Jesus. Pope John Paul II understood this well. This
devotion to Mary did not diminish or alter in any way the fundamental truth
that all faith points to God and the salvation brought by His only Son,
Jesus. Pope John Paul II understood that extremely well, too.

In revitalizing the Church, many followed the Pope into religious life.
It was Pope John Paul II that established the theme for these reflections on
the lives of the saints when speaking to a group of young seminarians. He

told them to Be Still, Be Not Afraid. Following Jesus is not something to fear, but something to cherish and hold to tightly.

There is a wonderful painting in Rome by Caravaggio titled "The Calling of Saint Matthew." It shows the young tax collector in his shop haggling with people over their tax bills. Jesus walks in and looks at him. He then extends His hand and motions for Matthew to follow. The others point at Saint Matthew as if to say, "There he is" and "You want him and not us." With head downcast, the look on Matthew's face is one of surprise and trepidation, but at the call of the Lord, he follows.

Like Matthew, the Lord calls each one of us to follow Him. The path He has chosen for us to follow may be very different, but it is one that will bring fullness to our lives and lead us to heaven. We will have the opportunity to share the Gospel with many along the way, so they too may hear God's call in their lives and join us on our journey. That is what Pope John Paul II experienced in his extraordinary life.

As Christ's Vicar on Earth, Pope John Paul II reintroduced the world to the love of Jesus. He set the stage for "a new springtime of Christianity." We must be the light that overcomes the darkness of our times so the beauty within each person can shine forth. We must answer God's call and live as if we are indeed proud of the Gospel of Jesus Christ.

Chapter 10

IT IS IMPORTANT to remember that all are called to follow Christ. It is also important to remember that God gives up on no one and redemption is offered to everyone, regardless of our sins. It requires our conversion, our turning to and commitment to follow Jesus, and if we do, He will give us all we need to walk a path of righteousness.

SAINT AUGUSTINE OF HIPPO
(September 2007)

Most of us have, at one time or another, shaken our heads at someone, a co-worker, a child, our spouse, and said, at least to ourselves, "it's about time." Many are not very patient as they wait for someone to "get with the program." Fortunately, God is patient and keeps calling to us, quietly and lovingly, to follow Him, as is evident from the life of Saint Augustine of Hippo, the patron saint of our diocese. When Augustine finally turned his life over to Jesus, God showed that He had great things in store for him. The people of his day and people throughout history, including us today, have benefited from his preaching and example.

Saint Augustine was born in 354 in Thagaste, a Roman town in Numidia, North Africa, what is modern day Algeria. He was the oldest of three children. His father was a pagan, but his mother, Saint Monica, was a devout Catholic. Augustine was sent to school in Madaura, a prosperous city 30 miles away until he was 15 years old. There, he became steeped in the pagan philosophies and excessive living of the city. Augustine was without supervision and fell for every temptation there was, following his father's example of getting the most out of life by whatever means presented themselves.

At the age of 17, Augustine went to Carthage to continue his studies in rhetoric. The city was a center for learning and lustful living in North Africa and Augustine was excited about both. Augustine was a gifted student and highly acclaimed. During this time, he developed a relationship with a woman with whom he would live for the next 15 years, fathering a son, but never marrying.

While in Carthage, Augustine became engrossed with the Manichee movement, a group whose philosophy recognized a good and evil spirit and held that sin was just part of who we are, so don't worry about it. That made his living a life without concern for the consequences easier. Augustine read everything, from pagan philosophers to the Bible, but none of it won him over.

Augustine began to teach and later returned to his home town to open a school. He grew restless and felt that a move to Rome would be best for him. His mother was against it, so he snuck out without telling anyone and traveled to Rome in 383. Upon his arrival, he met with illness and had difficulty setting up a school. When he did have students, they fled when it came time to pay, leaving Augustine without the funds necessary to carry on in the lifestyle to which he had been accustomed. Then he heard of an opening in Milan, the center of all academic thought and teaching. He applied for and won the job.

It was in Milan that his mother caught up with him, as did his son. As important, Augustine met Saint Ambrose, the Bishop of Milan. At first, Augustine wanted to hear Saint Ambrose preach, hoping to point out faults in his logic or argument, but rather, he became captivated. Augustine soon realized he needed to settle down and get married. He called off the 15 year relationship he had been living in and became engaged to a local girl by an arrangement with her family. When he had to wait two years to marry, he immediately took up with another woman. During this time, Augustine uttered his famous prayer, "Grant me chastity and continence, but not yet."

Augustine held the most esteemed academic position in the Latin world. But one day upon returning from a speech to the Emperor, the cheers of the crowd no longer satisfied his desires. He saw a drunken man in the streets acting quite merry, and Augustine wondered why he could not live so carefree.

All the while, Augustine and Saint Ambrose were becoming friends. One day, the saint told Augustine how fortunate he was to have a mother such as Monica who prayed constantly for her wayward son. This stuck with him. Also, the peaceful contentment on the faces of the people in prayer made Augustine long for what they had. Still, it was too easy to hang on to those things that kept him from God, yet his heart desired to follow in the footsteps of the apostles. He later wrote that he promised God that he would turn to Him in "a little while" and his "little while lasted a long time." This constant battle of wills finally came to a breaking point.

Augustine sought out Simplicianious, Saint Ambrose's confessor, and told him of his internal strife. Simplicianious told Augustine of the nobility of the truth and of sacrifice. He told him of the courage of those who preceded Augustine in following Jesus.

Augustine returned home and was sitting out in his garden, in tears. He cried out, "How long? How long shall this be? It is always tomorrow and tomorrow. Why not this hour an end to all my meanness?" Then he heard a small boy singing a nursery rhyme, the refrain of which was "Take up and read, take up and read." Augustine picked up the book he had with him of Saint Paul's letters and opened it randomly. It fell open at the *Letter to the Romans*, Chapter 13. He began reading at verse 12: "Let us throw off the works of darkness and put on the armor of light; let us conduct ourselves properly as in the day, not in rioting and drunkenness; not in sexual excess and lust; not in quarreling and jealousy. Rather, put on the Lord Jesus Christ and make no provision for the desires of the flesh."

The year was 386. Augustine was 31 years old. He and his son were baptized the next year at the Easter Vigil by Saint Ambrose. He was going to give up everything, his intended marriage, his position in Milan, and live a life of prayer and quiet. His plans, however, would not go exactly as he thought.

During his return trip to Africa, his mother died. His son would die soon afterwards. Arriving back in Thagaste, Augustine turned his family home into a monastery, giving what he had to the poor. He had no thoughts of becoming a priest, and no desire if asked. But in those days, the people could make one a priest, and that is just what happened to Augustine in 391. One day, while praying in a church in Hippo, the people surrounded him and demanded the bishop ordain him a priest. And so it came to pass.

Augustine, well known for his rhetoric from before, became even better known as a preacher. He was named auxiliary bishop of the diocese of Hippo in 396, becoming Bishop shortly thereafter, a position he would hold until his death.

During his 34 years as bishop, Augustine would continue to preach, daily or twice daily, write (he is the most voluminous writer of his time), and combat heresy. He debated leaders of the Manichees, thoroughly denouncing their error and winning them over to Christianity. He combated several other false teachings concerning Jesus and the Church. Finally, in his later years, when all he wanted was a little time to pray and write, the Arian heresy arose. They spread their beliefs and influence with violence, ultimately invading Hippo. It was during this invasion that Saint Augustine died in his sleep on August 28, 430.

His entire life was spent in search of the truth, for only that would sustain him. Saint Augustine finally realized on that night in Milan that the truth he sought was Jesus. He wrote: "Thou hast made us, O Lord, for thyself, and our heart shall find no rest till it rest in thee." His long journey to this realization is summed up in these words: "Late have I loved you, O Beauty ever ancient, ever new, late have I loved you? You were within me, but I was outside, and it was there that I searched for you. ... You called, you shouted, and you broke through my deafness. You flashed, you shone, and you dispelled my blindness. ... You touched me, and I burned for your peace." That peace he sought was realized when he turned his life over to Christ and followed him, as did Saint Paul, serving him in the priesthood and preaching the Gospel.

There are three things in particular to take from the life of Saint Augustine. First, we find no real peace until our lives belong to God.

Second, our faith compels us to know and defend our faith when others teach philosophies that are contrary to Church teaching. We cannot sit back and remain silent. Third, no matter the things we have done in life, it is never too late to turn our lives over to God and follow Jesus. He will wait patiently for us, but we should not make Him wait. He may have a special blessing for you as a priest or a sister. To hear Him, like Saint Augustine, we must Be Still ... Be Not Afraid. To What is Jesus Calling You?

* * *

Saint Augustine was very involved in refuting the Arian heresy. During his time, there was a powerful group of people promoting the notion that Jesus was not divine from the beginning, but was raised to the divine due to his life. Such a false proclamation proved dangerous in its confusion to people on the true nature of Christ. As we know from Scripture and the teaching of the apostles, Jesus is the only begotten Son of the Father. God, three persons but one God has always been, and Jesus as the Second Person of the Most Holy Trinity has always been. It was the mystery of the Trinity that was intertwined with the refutation of the Arian heresy, and there is a famous story involving Saint Augustine and his trying to understand and find a way of properly articulating the doctrine of the Trinity.

As the story goes, one day Saint Augustine was walking on the beach. He saw a boy scooping out the water and pouring it into a hole. Saint Augustine asked him what he was doing and the boy said he was trying to empty the ocean. Saint Augustine laughed and told him it was impossible to empty the ocean into the hole. In response, the boy said it was equally impossible to fully grasp the mystery of the Trinity.

Combating heresy involved not just theological debate, but confronting political force and at times being subjected to threats of violence. Still, Saint Augustine stood steadfast in preaching the truth of Jesus Christ. The Church formally resolved and answered the Arian heresy at the Council of Nicaea as reflected in the resulting Nicene Creed. In it, which we profess every time we go to Mass, we proclaim Jesus as "God from God, light from light, true God from true God, begotten not made, consubstantial with the Father, through him all things were made." In other words, Jesus has coexisted with the Father and the Holy Spirit for all eternity and will continue to exist for all time. Jesus is "the Word made flesh," the Word that was there "in the beginning" as we hear in Saint John's Gospel.

Saint Augustine lived his life in search of the Truth, finally discovering there was but one Truth, the Truth to which Jesus testified, the Truth that was Jesus Himself, the Son of God. We often try to find meaning for our lives in the things of the world, finding that they do not hold up when put to the test. Our hearts desire peace, but we only find true peace when we encounter the Prince of Peace. Carefree living, exotic travel, high status, and the like are fleeting and fail to serve as a foundation for life. Saint Augustine discovered this in much the same way as the prodigal son.

Saint Augustine's life is an example of the promise of redemption and the joy that comes when we know and live the teachings of the Gospel. Saint Augustine teaches us how destructive sin is to our souls, but if we repent and turn to Jesus, we will fill the emptiness sin creates. He tells us that we have a God-shaped hole in our soul that only a love of God can fill. It is Jesus who is the Way, the Truth, and the Life and all of the pleasures, treasures, or honors of the world do nothing to bring us to heaven, which is where our soul will find true joy, true peace. We get there when our soul rests in the Lord, as Saint Augustine found out. He had to follow Jesus, even if he wanted a little more time to play with the vices of this world. When he finally chose to follow Jesus, Saint Augustine realized that he should have chosen that path much sooner, for it was only when he followed Jesus that he found true happiness.

Chapter 11

WHEN CHRISTMAS ROLLED around again, my focus turned
to the silent but necessary witness, Saint Joseph. Saint Joseph faced many
challenges by being pulled into a vocation he never expected and probably
feared. Just as Mary was in awe and confused by God's call, Saint Joseph
was equally confused by being asked to accept Mary's pregnancy and the
role they were about to play in the salvation of mankind.

SAINT JOSEPH
(December 2007)

Sometimes, things do not go exactly as planned. Life will throw us a curve
ball every now and then. At times, we discover that what we thought we
were getting into is nothing like what we expected. Faith tells us that if we
choose our path out of service and love of God, then God will create good
out of the twists, turns, and obstacles we must face. Saint Joseph must have
wondered a number of times after being betrothed to Mary what he had
gotten himself into, but he trusted that God had it figured out and stayed
the course.

We know little of Saint Joseph beyond what we learn in Matthew's and
Luke's Gospels. We do not know where he was born, when or how he died,
how old he was when he married Mary, or many other things we would like
to know. He was clearly a righteous man from the House of King David

who loved God and kept his laws. Joseph was not present for Jesus' public ministry, but how long before Jesus began His ministry Joseph died, we do not know. Yet, what we do know should bring us comfort and encouragement when facing the unknown and clearly difficult situations in life.

Joseph was engaged to be married to Mary, who was an early teen at the time. He must have been excited and anticipating his upcoming marriage. It was then he discovered, most likely from Mary herself, that she was pregnant. Young girls who got pregnant before they were married, especially if the groom was not the father, did not make ideal wives, particularly for someone as devout as Saint Joseph. Yet here, we get the first glimpse of Saint Joseph's heart.

Saint Joseph could have denounced Mary and subjected her to much ridicule and possibly even stoning. No one would have believed her story of the Annunciation, that she had become pregnant by the power of the Holy Spirit as foretold by an angel. But Joseph wanted to spare Mary the public humiliation and scorn, so he decided to divorce her quietly, which would have led to her exile, but at least not her execution.

Before doing so, he had a dream where an angel told him not to worry about taking Mary for his wife, for her child was conceived by the power of the Holy Spirit. It was Joseph's responsibility to name him Jesus, for the child would save his people from their sins. As strange of a dream as that may seem, Joseph trusted God and took Mary into his home. He was then faced with a young, pregnant wife and a prophecy about his soon to be son, which he could not possibly understand.

As if his circumstances could not have gotten any more off track, Caesar announced that all were to return to their home city to be registered as part of a census. This would also help with taxes, which the very modest, if not poor Joseph would have a hard time paying. Furthermore, his new wife was about to give birth. Still, they made the journey from Galilee to Bethlehem, as required, only to find the city overrun with people and no room for them at the inn. He found a stable, most likely born out of rock, and settled his wife in to what would become their home for the next several months.

From here, Joseph was continually amazed. When Jesus was born, people from all around, beginning with shepherds out in the fields, came to see the child and worship him. They told stories of angels announcing his birth. Then, three kings or astrologers from far off lands arrived bearing gifts he could never afford, gold, frankincense, and myrrh. They worshipped the child and called him the King of the Jews, a title King Herod would not have approved, and one the Romans would scoff at.

In accordance with the law, after eight days, Joseph and Mary took Jesus to the Temple to be offered to God as he was their first born. Being unable to afford a lamb, they purchased two pigeons or doves for the sacrificial offering. When he presented the child to the old priest, Simeon, Joseph was again stunned by what he heard. In giving praise to God, Simeon said "With my own eyes I have seen your salvation, which you have prepared in the presence of all peoples: A light to reveal your will to the Gentiles and bring glory to your people Israel." Simeon then told Mary, "This child is chosen by God for the destruction and the salvation of many in Israel. He will be a sign from God which many people will speak against and so reveal their secret thoughts. And sorrow, like a sharp sword, will break your own heart." So too, an old woman, Anna, upon seeing the child, cried out that she had now seen the one who would set Jerusalem free. In a city under Roman rule, such a proclamation could only mean trouble for Joseph and his family.

Indeed, trouble was not far off, but again, Joseph was warned in a dream of Herod's anger at the birth of a Messiah, and so, in accordance with the angel's instructions, he fled with Mary and Jesus to Egypt. He could not go into hiding, but had to flee to a foreign land, the same land where his ancestors had been enslaved, and waited for the death of King Herod. Several years later, he was told in another dream that King Herod had died, so Joseph packed up his family to returned to Israel, where they settled in Nazareth.

Joseph worked as a carpenter, providing for his family as best he could. He kept the commandments, and traveled to Jerusalem to celebrate the Passover. When Jesus was 12 years old, he stayed behind, while his family and others from their town started heading home. A day into the journey, Mary and Joseph discovered that the boy was missing, and the heart of a father must have broken. They searched three days for Jesus, finally finding him in the Temple surrounded by the teachers of the law, who were listening intently to his young son. Again, he had to be in wonder of God's plan, for it certainly was not the one he expected when he decided to become Mary's husband.

This is the last time Saint Joseph appears in the Gospels. He does not speak a word in all of Scripture, but he speaks volumes in how he responds, without question or hesitation to God's call. We do not get the neon signposts of angels speaking to us in our dreams to know what God's will is for us. But then again, I'm not sure we would find our dreams to be those signposts we want when asked to follow what appears to be a very difficult road to travel. Nevertheless, God has a plan for each of us, just as he did with Saint Joseph. We, like him, must be willing to listen to God speaking to us and then do His will, regardless of the circumstances. The joy and amazement that will follow us as we walk the path God selects will make the trepidation all worth it, even if that path leads to the priesthood or religious life. So Be Still, Be Not Afraid, To What is Jesus Calling You?

* * *

If we walk the path God lays out for us, and Saint Joseph did just that, the wonders we will experience are beyond our imagination. There may be times when we will want to run the other direction or ask to get off the ride we are on, but if we truly follow Christ, the impossible will become the marvelous. From the perspective of hindsight, it is easy to see that Saint Joseph made the right choice in life. But we do not get to see our lives with the benefit of hindsight when a choice is presented to us. We are called to trust in the Lord, follow Him and be faithful to His teachings.

Saint Joseph is the ever faithful if silent rock behind Jesus' childhood. He worked hard to provide for his family financially, spiritually, and emotionally. By any standards, life for this new family was hard. Yet, through it all, we know nothing to suggest Saint Joseph was not the perfect father, the perfect husband. While appropriately honored, he still remains in the shadows. His example is that we do not need the limelight to do the work of Christ. We do not need to be the center of attention. His joy came from Mary and Jesus. He stayed the course and knew that his life was a testament of his faith and God's goodness. When Mother Teresa said that we are not called to be successful, we are called to be faithful, she could not have found a better example than Saint Joseph. This quiet man was truly faithful until God called him home for the best seat in the house for watching the ministry of salvation come to the world.

Chapter 12

CATHOLIC EDUCATION IS the epitome of how we as a people of faith provide our children with the information they need to be successful in the world and to grow in their Catholic faith. A fundamental tenet of Catholic education is how our faith should form how we live in the world. Life will challenge our faith. Yet, with a strong faith foundation, we can face any obstacle that life may throw at us.

We constantly face challenges where one or more of the options available violate our faith. The question is how we choose between those options when the popular or easy out would run contrary to our faith. We may encounter instances where we are questioned or ridiculed for our faith, whether from a lack of understanding of Church teaching or in response to the sins of some within the Church or from a general rejection of God's existence. The question is how we respond to such questioning or ridicule. Being directly challenged is not easy, but the Lord promised that if we held on to Him, if we followed Him, He would lead us through such times and give us the words to speak.

Nothing can change or diminish the truth of Christ's teaching as it has been handed down to us from the apostles. Remaining steadfast in the Truth is worth rejection from family, friends, and country, for only Jesus leads us to the promise of heaven. We experience that Truth within the Church, even with the faults that we bring to the Church as sinners. We will not always have all the answers, but we are called to grow in understanding and knowledge of our faith so that we can grow closer to the Lord and pass on our faith to others. As Church, we walk this road together knowing that we are never alone in our quest for a greater understanding and love of God.

Saint Elizabeth Ann Seton had a choice to make when she came to know the truth of the Church's teaching. She had to worry about how her children would be treated, whether she could find work to provide for them, and whether she would still be welcome in her family and town. But Saint Elizabeth Ann Seton chose to follow Jesus no matter the rejection she suffered and in doing so, she realized the importance of teaching our children about God's truth while preparing them for life. Little did she know that in following her heart, she would found a religious order as a widowed mother of five and begin a school system that would become the largest parochial education system in the nation. Because of Saint Elizabeth Ann Seton, children of all generations have had the chance to obtain a top notch education while learning about their faith and what it means to be a follower of Jesus in today's world.

SAINT ELIZABETH ANN SETON
(January 2008)

Being challenged because of your faith can be very uncomfortable. Many of us have probably been asked questions about what we believe as Catholics and why, sometimes by well meaning people and sometimes by those critical of Church teaching. But, in defense of our faith, the truth about God, Jesus, and His love for us, would we be willing to be ostracized by our family and considered an outcast by our friends? Would we, when given the opportunity, move to a new place with our children and start a ministry that would transform a nation? That is the story of Saint Elizabeth Ann Seton.

Elizabeth was born August 28, 1774, on the outskirts of New York City. She was the second child of Dr. Richard Bayley and his first wife Catherine Charlton Bayley. Dr. Bayley was the first Medical Officer of New York and was instrumental in getting the city through epidemics of yellow fever. Her mother died when Elizabeth was two, while giving birth to Elizabeth's younger sister.

Dr. Bayley remarried when Elizabeth was 4, but her relationship with her new stepmother was cool at best. Dr. Bayley and his new wife had 7 children of their own. Elizabeth and her older sister, Mary, were so unwelcome that they spent several years with her uncle. Elizabeth, however, had a very close relationship with her father and their letters to each other brought comfort to both during his trips away from New York. Dr. Bayley ultimately died of the plague in 1801, with Elizabeth bringing him comfort in his final hours.

As she got older, Elizabeth helped with her younger siblings, took part in the social scene of New York, and remained a faithful communicant at Trinity Episcopal Church. She was, in all things, a Christian in the Episcopal tradition.

Elizabeth took the normal interest in guys. Ultimately, she fell in love with a young man, William Seton, whose father ran a merchant marine business. On January 25, 1794, in her sister's home, Elizabeth and William were married. Elizabeth and Will were very much in love. They would eventually have five children.

The first four years of their marriage were happy and care free. Then, in 1798, her father-in-law passed away. This left Elizabeth and Will to help raise his seven youngest brothers and sisters. The strain on the family was immense. The young mother who already had three small children of her own now had seven additional children to raise. Will, on the other hand, was not the business man his father was and the business crumbled, leaving the family constantly on the verge of bankruptcy by Christmas 1799.

By 1803, Will was suffering greatly, both physically and financially, and he wanted to travel to Italy in hopes of getting a new lease on his health. The trip would be his last, and Elizabeth's first steps on her journey toward Catholicism.

Will had business friends in Leghorn, Italy, the Filicchis. The two brothers were good to him and were anticipating his arrival. In October 1803, Elizabeth, Will, and their oldest child, Ann Maria, set sail for Italy. Their other children stayed with relatives. They arrived in Leghorn on November 18, 1803, but due to concerns of illness, all three Setons were locked up in a drafty prison on the coast for 30 days in quarantine.

On December 19, 1803, the Setons left the prison and headed to Antonio Filicchi's home. Eight days later, Will died. Elizabeth's mourning was in the home of new found friends, friends she had no way of knowing would lead her to God's plan for her. The Filicchis were devout Catholics. Elizabeth spent time in the churches in the area and was taken in by their beauty. Antonio told her of Catholic teaching on the Eucharist and the sacraments. Elizabeth was moved by what she heard, knowing that her yearning for God could not be filled with her own faith tradition. Even the sign of the cross left her in awe. Still, Elizabeth was born and raised Episcopalian, and the anti-Catholic sentiment of New York left Elizabeth confused.

Elizabeth returned home a widow, but found all her children to be in good health. Elizabeth, however, remained unsettled in faith. She corresponded with Antonio and his wife often. They asked her only to pray and inquire regarding the faith. When Elizabeth spoke of her spiritual crisis and interest in Catholicism with friends and family, she was met with ridicule and disbelief. Her family expressed concern for her children and over her association with the youngest Setons, Cecilia and Harriett, whom she loved and had raised as her own daughters. Cecilia and Harriett were later forbidden from seeing Elizabeth due to her conversion.

The pressures were difficult as she discerned her future over the next nine months. Elizabeth lost weight, prayed fervently, and those she needed most were not in New York. People grew weary of her comments and Catholic leanings. Even Henry Hobart, her long time minister and friend who was instrumental in her faith life, gave Elizabeth many anti-Catholic books to read and tried to dissuade her from her fancy. When his efforts failed, he broke off contact with her. Upon her conversion, Hobart warned people to disassociate from her. This greatly impacted Elizabeth when she had the chance to work in a private boarding school, as people were led to fear that she would attempt to convert their children to Catholicism.

On Ash Wednesday 1805, Elizabeth went to Saint Peter's Catholic Church in New York. Elizabeth wrote Mrs. Filicchi: "Entering it, how the heart died away as it were in silence before the little tabernacle and the great crucifixion over it." She submitted to the Church on March 14, 1805. Six days later, she made her first confession, noting "I felt as if my chains fell, as those of Saint Peter at the touch of the divine Messenger. My God, what new scenes for my soul!" Five days later, amid much anticipation, Elizabeth received her first Communion, with her final acceptance into the Church on Easter 1805.

Elizabeth had obvious concerns for her children. She wanted them to learn and appreciate their new faith, but worried about the pressures others would put on them as a result of their mother's conversion. After dealing with rejection from friends and family and much consideration, Elizabeth finally accepted an invitation to go to Baltimore in 1808 where she was to help in a school. While she found a welcoming environment for her family in Baltimore, Elizabeth worried about Cecilia and Harriett. Left behind in New York, their family continued to put mounting pressure on both girls, trying to isolate them from Elizabeth, even screening letters between them and Elizabeth.

In Baltimore, Elizabeth's long held desire for religious life would be realized. Elizabeth met priests who would help her in her spiritual development. She also met a wealthy convert, Samuel Cooper, who was studying for the priesthood. Their mutual desire for a religious vocation kept their relationship from becoming something other than mutual admiration and respect.

God brought them together because their hearts desired the same thing. Cooper and Elizabeth both told their spiritual director of their desire to build a religious community with a school that would teach children the foundations of their faith in addition to the things they needed to know to be successful in the world. While Elizabeth desired the religious life, she would not do anything that took her away from her primary responsibility of being a mother to her children. Cooper would put up the money, but wanted Elizabeth to be the head of the Community, the Daughters of Charity, a position that earned her the title of "Mother." This, of course, is something she did very well.

Elizabeth and four other young women made their vows of poverty, chastity, and obedience on March 25, 1809, the Feast of the Annunciation. Upon putting on her habit, Elizabeth uttered this prayer, "My gracious God! You know my unfitness for this task. I, who by my sins have so often crucified you. I blush with shame and confusion. How can I teach others, who know so little myself, and am so miserable and imperfect?" To her delight, Cecilia and Harriett Seton joined them later that summer.

The Daughters of Charity would start their school in Emmitsburg, a small community at the foot of Mount Saint Mary about 50 miles from Baltimore. Elizabeth and her six sisters lived in a small log house until the larger home was built. On February 22, 1810, Elizabeth opened the first Catholic School in the United States. Her model proved to be the model used in establishing Catholic schools all over the country. The sisters opened hospitals, orphanages, and parochial schools throughout the Northeast. This is why Elizabeth Ann Seton is known as the Mother of Catholic Education in the United States. She wanted to make sure the children understood the fullness of their faith, how God was truly present to them in the sacraments, and the treasure of the Church's teachings that come to us from the apostles.

Elizabeth Ann Seton died on January 4, 1821, and was canonized on September 14, 1975, the first native born American to be named a saint. Her life is one of constantly following the will of God and desiring to know and love Him more fully. She took joy in nothing else. She suffered persecution for her faith by those she held most dear, but her love of God and her experience of Christ within the Catholic Church were enough to carry her through. She endured great suffering only to find great reward in accepting God's call in her life. We too benefit from her answer to God's call. Are we willing to do the same and follow Him regardless of what others think and say? If our faith is founded on Christ and not the approval of others, then we will. To hear God's call and survive the challenges that will surely come, especially for those who chose the priesthood or religious life, we must Be Still, Be Not Afraid ... To What is Jesus Calling You?

* * *

Peace comes from following Christ, from doing His will in our life. All other pressures, challenges, and temptations are not relevant because Christ calls us to focus on Him. He said being a disciple may pit mother against daughter and father against son and to take a stand for Christ in the face of disapproval from family is incredibly difficult. Yet, some are called to be that strong and Jesus will give you the strength if that is the path you must walk. Our salvation is the most important and with that, we find peace.

Many saints were rejected in their own time by those closest to them. Saint Elizabeth Ann Seton should inspire us to keep our eyes on Christ. In the end, those most important to her followed her because through her they heard the voice of the one true Sheppard. Upon hearing His voice, they were compelled to set out to do His will no matter where it took them because He was with them always just as He promised.

Saint Elizabeth Ann Seton experienced the fullness of Christ's love in her receiving the Eucharist. She discovered that His command and His promise in the upper room on the night before he died was not figurative. Rather, Jesus' command to "do this" was to share in His true presence in the Eucharist. It was His promise that He would be with us now and always, truly with us. Just as the bread and wine became the actual Body and Blood, Soul and Divinity of Jesus at the Last Supper, so it does for us at each Mass. As the disciples came to know Him on the road to Emmaus in "the breaking of the bread," so we come to truly know and experience Jesus in the Eucharist.

It has been said that if Catholics truly believed what is taught about the Eucharist, we would approach the altar each Sunday with fear and trepidation. We do not approach the altar for a bit of bread and a sip of wine to merely remember Jesus. He said for us to "do this," which was to take and eat the flesh of the Son of Man and drink His blood that was spilled to bring salvation to the world, an act He said would bring us life eternal with Him. We were not asked to do a reenactment, but to share in the reality of that moment that is re-experienced, not just remembered at Mass. We experience Jesus living and true in the Eucharist and cannot help but become transformed by the Bread of Life and Cup of Eternal Salvation, for it is Jesus we receive, not a symbol of Him.

Saint Elizabeth Ann Seton came to know this truth and with that knowledge flowed countless other truths that come to us from Jesus. He taught His disciples the wonders of God's love. His call to us is for the conversion of our souls, a repentance of sins. Through the sacraments, we experience His love and His grace in extraordinary ways. We receive forgiveness of sins in the sacrament of reconciliation. We walk with the prodigal son toward our father's house only to find the father running out to meet us. We must drop to our knees as the prodigal son did and confess our sins and receive our Father's forgiveness. The sacrament of reconciliation allows us to hear those words of absolution, knowing that Jesus' words again ring true that the sins the disciples forgive are forgiven and those they hold bound are held bound. That ministry is passed to the priest who administers the sacrament for the salvation of our souls and prepares us to meet Jesus in the Eucharist and on our Judgment Day.

Saint Elizabeth Ann Seton knew that with her acceptance of all Jesus taught, she would become an outcast in a city that feared and ostracized the Catholic Church. But as she was walking in at the sound of the bells to meet her Savior face to face, no amount of rejection from others was going to keep her from following Jesus. She is truly one who sold everything she had to buy that fine pearl. Whether we have come to faith only recently or were blessed with the gift of faith from our childhood, we must never let go of that precious gift. Like Saint Elizabeth Ann Seton, we must follow the Lord wherever He calls us and listen to His voice, not the voice of the crowd. The voice of the crowd condemned Jesus to death, and it is the voice of Jesus that calls us to new life.

Saint Elizabeth Ann Seton came to realize that a complete education had to involve learning and studying our faith. Only by learning more about our faith will we see it grow. The more she learned about the Catholic faith, the more her heart burned to learn more and the closer she became to Jesus. Study and prayer must accompany the sacraments to nurture the graces we receive in the sacraments. To develop the faith we need for daily living requires more than one hour in church on Sunday. To prepare ourselves and our children for life, we must study more than literature, math, science, history, and other subjects. We must also study and learn about our faith for our education to be complete.

Our faith is an indispensable part of life, of who we are as Christians. Keeping Jesus in the midst of our studies reminds us that as we grow older, Jesus is in the midst of our work, our play, our family. That is the blessing of Catholic Education; we get to prepare our children for the whole of life as disciples of Jesus Christ.

Chapter 13

WHILE THE PURPOSE of these talks was to encourage religious vocations, the important thing is to listen to God and follow Him wherever He is calling us to serve. Not everyone is called to a religious vocation, but we should all be open to whatever our calling may be, whatever our vocation may be. Saint Elizabeth Ann Seton married and had children before being called to a religious vocation upon her conversion to Catholicism following her husband's death. Likewise, Saint Thomas More was married with children when he was called upon to make a perfect statement of faith through his public service. He is a great example of placing principle before politics and God before temporal desires. He discovered through prayer that he was not being called to a religious vocation, but he would stand up for Christ as a faithful disciple in the public arena. He lived his vocation faithfully to the very end.

SAINT THOMAS MORE
(March 2008)

For most of us, we will never be given the choice of rejecting the Church's teaching and authority to avoid being imprisoned and executed. Yet, many freely reject the Church's teaching on particular matters when it suits them. For Saint Thomas More, a loyal servant of the King of England, when he was given a choice between Church and King, he chose to follow his

conscience rather than the request of the King. The result was his behead-
ing, and his subsequent canonization.

Thomas More was born February 7, 1478, the second of six children
born to John and Agnes More of London, England. His father started as a
butler, but worked his way up to becoming a Judge of the King's Bench.
His study and lofty position in the law ultimately led Thomas down a similar path.

Thomas attended top schools in London. After two years at Oxford,
Thomas entered the New Inn in 1494 to begin his studies in the law. He
was to be a lawyer like his father. His legal studies, however, were not his
primary interest and they did not take him away from his study of the early
Church Fathers, particularly Saint Augustine.

From 1497 to 1501, Thomas lived near the Carthusian monastery and
practiced their discipline. It was during this time that Thomas considered
very seriously becoming a priest and religious. While he ultimately decided
to remain a layperson, the discipline of the Carthusians never left him, including his wearing of a hair shirt under his clothes, his attendance at daily
Mass, his offering of the Divine Office, and his works of penance, fasting,
and abstinence.

By choosing to remain a layperson, Thomas confronted the challenges
everyday life presented to a way of spirituality. This may have led to his
translation of the biography of the then recently deceased Italian scholar
Giovanni Pico della Mirandola, a man of great spirituality who remained an
unmarried layperson. Thomas found comfort and more than a little parallel
between his life and that of John Picus, as the name was translated. Thomas
was convinced of the importance of having holy people work in positions
of public import, such as the law and government. He knew that by remaining faithful to Church teaching and following Christ, he would face
obstacles and ridicule, but if that was his calling, he would prepare himself
as best he could in study and devotion.

In 1504, Thomas was elected a burgess in Parliament. His career in
politics got off to a noticeable start. Thomas committed what many would
consider political suicide when he gave voice and ultimately prevailed in
opposing the reigning king, Henry VII's request for significant public finan-
cial support for the wedding of his daughter to the King of Scotland. Henry

wanted 60,000 pounds, but had to settle for 30,000, and was not very amused. As a result, Thomas's father was imprisoned in the Tower of London until he paid a fine of 100 pounds. Henry VII's anger with Thomas did not subside until the king died in 1509, to be succeeded by his 18-year-old son Henry VIII.

In 1505, Thomas asked for the hand of Jane Colt in marriage. She was the oldest of three sisters. They would have four children, three girls and one boy. His friend, Erasmus, described Thomas More as follows: "His hair is dark brown or brownish black. The eyes are grayish blue. ... In a word, if you want a perfect model of friendship, you will find it in no one better than More. ... In human affairs there is nothing from which he does not extract enjoyment, even from things that are most serious. If he converses with the learned and judicious, he delights in their talent, if with the ignorant and foolish, he enjoys their stupidity. He is not even offended by professional jesters. With a wonderful dexterity he accommodates himself to every disposition. As a rule, in talking with women, even with his own wife, he is full of jokes and banter. No one is less led by the opinions of the crowd, yet no one departs less from common sense."

In 1510, Thomas was appointed to the post of under-sheriff for London, acting as legal advisor to the mayor and sheriffs of the city. Thomas appeared in court on Thursdays to hear cases, which left him plenty of time for his own studies and writings.

In 1511, his wife, then only 23-years-old, fell ill and died. Thomas would not leave his children without a mother for long, remarrying 30 days later to Alice Middleton, a widow seven years his senior with several children of her own, but one still young enough to join the household with Thomas's four young children.

Thomas was taken into the close counsel of Henry VIII, who would often visit Thomas at his home. The king sent Thomas on several diplomatic missions to other countries. In 1521, Thomas was knighted and made sub-treasurer to the king. In 1523, he was elected Speaker of the House of Commons. Then, in 1529, he was selected as Lord Chancellor of England, a post he would hold until his resignation in 1532 due to his disagreement with the king's and parliament's usurpation of Church authority.

Thomas was fiercely loyal to the Church, even if he disagreed with the actions of certain members of the clergy. He held Christian unity as dear and as desired by Christ. He held the Church's doctrines of faith as inviolate and necessary of protection. He showed little tolerance for heretics.

When Martin Luther nailed his 95 theses to the door of the church in Wittenburg and the Protestant Reformation was begun, Thomas More was thrown into the middle of it, writing a number of refutations to the reformers' new theology and defenses of Church teaching. Ironically, one work Thomas found influential was written by King Henry VIII in defense of the seven sacraments, a work that also contained a strong defense of papal authority.

The king's defense of the Church would change within five years of his writing this work, however, for he wanted to annul his marriage to marry another, a move not approved by the Church. Given the Church's disapproval, the king took a different view of papal authority, ultimately using parliament to declare that the pope exercised no authority in England, and the king was the sole authority for Church and State. These actions drove a wedge between Thomas and his king.

The story of King Henry VIII's battle with the Church over his divorce from his wife of 20 years is a long one. He sought to divorce her, at least in part, because she did not give him a male heir. It resulted in the prior Lord Chancellor being deposed and Thomas More being selected to follow him, the first layman to hold the position. Henry's moves against the Church began with a royal proclamation ordering the clergy to acknowledge him as "Supreme Head" of the Church "as far as the law of God will permit." Without an annulment, Henry proceeded to marry Anne Boleyn and then forced a succession act through parliament, which required all who were called upon to swear an oath acknowledging the children of Henry and Anne as legitimate heirs to the throne and repudiating "any foreign authority, prince or potentate," specifically the pope. During the annulment controversy, parliament also outlawed any referral of a dispute within the Church to Rome for resolution as it conflicted with the king's sovereign authority.

Thomas More attempted to remain neutral on the king's new marriage, at least in the public eye, after his resignation in May 1532. Even so, the first direct attack on Thomas came the following year when his name appeared on a bill of attainder suggesting that Thomas was guilty of treason for supporting the pope. When questioned regarding his stance on the king's recent marriage, Thomas only said that he had already explained his position to the king in person, and it had not brought about any displeasure. Ultimately, his name was removed from the bill.

Reprieve was not to last long. On April 14, 1534, Thomas was summoned to take the Act of Succession oath. Upon leaving his home, he knew he would not return. After being left to watch numerous people come before him and sign the oath without question or hesitation, it was finally Thomas's turn. He read the entire Act, and understanding the implication of rejecting all "foreign authority" meant rejecting papal authority over the Church and ecclesial matters, Thomas simply refused to sign. He was given time to rethink his position, but he still refused. Four days later, he was taken to the Tower of London, where he would remain for the next 15 months.

This time in Thomas's life was another time of great writing, especially on the suffering of Christ. He was allowed to correspond with his family and friends. Thomas More was ultimately brought up on charges of treason on July 1, 1535, convicted, and beheaded on July 6th. His body was buried, and according to royal decree, as with all those executed for his crime, his head was placed on London Bridge for a month.

Thomas More firmly believed that Jesus created one Church, governed not by monarchs or the whims of the time, but by a succession from Saint Peter, guided by the Holy Spirit. While some men who had held high office in the Church, including that of Pope, had committed great sin, that did not detract from the Truth of the Church's doctrines, which come from Christ Himself as handed down in Scripture and in the teachings of the Apostles. When given the choice of serving God and His Church or his king, Thomas chose God and His Church. He would not be swayed by the masses who blindly followed the will of the king, either out of fear of what would happen to them or ignorance of what their actions really meant. He died as he lived, "The King's Good Servant, but God's First."

We are given choices everyday on whether we will follow God or someone or something else. Most of those choices do not carry with them the loss of our heads, but over time, they could carry with them the loss of our souls. Like Thomas, are we willing to sacrifice everything to follow God, even if it should seem folly to others? Are we willing to spend time in prayer and fasting to discern what path God wishes for us to follow in life? It may be to the priesthood or religious life, or it may be to married life and one of service in the world, but we will not know unless we are willing to Be Still, Be Not Afraid, to What is Jesus Calling You?

* * *

In his second letter to Timothy, Saint Paul wrote: "For God did not give us a spirit of cowardice, but rather of power and love and self-control. So do not be ashamed of your testimony to our Lord, nor of me, a prisoner for his sake; but bear your share of hardship for the Gospel with the strength that comes from God. He saved us and called us to a holy life, not according to our works but according to his own design and the grace bestowed on us in Christ Jesus before time began, but now made manifest through the appearance of our savior Christ Jesus, who destroyed death and brought life and immortality to light through the Gospel, for which I was appointed preacher and apostle and teacher. On this account I am suffering these things; but I am not ashamed, for I know him in whom I have believed and am confident that he is able to guard what has been entrusted to me until that day." Saint Thomas More lived a life of strong faith with a spirit of power and love and self-control. He suffered for the sake of the Gospel, of remaining true to Jesus Christ. When given the choice between remaining loyal to Church teaching or to the contrary whims of his king, Saint Thomas More chose the same path as Saint Paul, he would stand with Christ.

Saint Thomas More's life should encourage each of us to stand up for our faith. For those who serve in public office, he should be an inspiration. He is the great example that public servants may be forced to choose between fidelity to Christ and public ambition, where choosing faith may cost one their position in public service. Scripture tells us to always choose our faith for it is a trade-off that is always worth it. Too often, we may profess Jesus as Lord, but publicly shy away from living and defending the Gospel.

While a public servant's job is not to force anyone to have a particular faith, it is a public servant's job to stand up for the truth and promote values and principles that we know serve the public good. A politician who says they have faith but cannot vote consistent with that faith is living a lie. Such politicians abandon their faith and a respect for life and wonder why the Church does not give them a pass for such cowardice. We know from Scripture that if we deny Christ, He will deny knowing us. We are called to be witnesses to the Truth, not to political ambition or to make someone like us. Jesus was rejected and many walked away finding it too difficult to follow Him. By doing so, they walked away from their own salvation. We cannot afford to do the same.

Saint Thomas understood that he had to be God's servant first. We need good, God-fearing people in public service. Saint Thomas was a great public servant. But as Scripture tells us, we can have only one master. When public service seeks our souls, we must stand up for truth. For it is better to lose our heads than our souls to the fires of Hell.

Chapter 14

WHETHER THEY ARE stances on big issues or small anonymous acts, all things should be done out of our love of Jesus. Faith affects all we do, it is how we live, and defines who we are. When our heart belongs to Christ, we see the needs of others and respond out of love. Our faith should define who we are and be the reason for all we do.

SAINT NICHOLAS
(December 2008)

It is amazing that random acts of kindness are often the things that leave the most lasting impression on people and bring the most satisfaction to those who do them. In a way, such small, unassuming acts of generosity are reflective of Christ's birth, an event virtually unnoticed at the time and completely humble in appearance. For one young man, bringing joy and hope to others without seeking any recognition, indeed, doing everything possible to be unnoticed, was his mode of operation. His random acts of kindness have had such an impact over the centuries that he is remembered across the globe for his holiness. Indeed, we cannot celebrate the birth of our Lord, whom he served with all he had, without remembering and celebrating this great saint.

Nicholas was born in the village of Patara near the port city of Myra in what is now Turkey sometime between 260 and 280. His parents were wealthy, but taught him the importance of caring for those less fortunate. Raised a Christian from birth, Nicholas remained steadfast in his faith throughout his life, even when Christians were routinely persecuted. Nicholas's parents died during an epidemic when he was very young. Rather than live a lavish lifestyle as his inheritance would have permitted, Nicholas chose another path, ultimately selling what he had and giving to the poor, the sick, and the needy.

Nicholas was known in Myra for his works of holiness. So much so, that when they needed a bishop, Nicholas, although a layman, was elected Bishop of Myra, a post he would hold until his death. Nicholas did not seek the position, but when those who gathered in the church to elect the next bishop prayed for guidance, Nicholas was the one who knocked on the door. Given his gentle and pious nature, it was clear to those in attendance that God had ordained that Nicholas would be their bishop.

Nicholas spoke out often in defense of the Gospel. He even went so far as to destroy the pagan temple of Artemis. During the persecutions of the Roman Emperor Diocletian, Nicholas was imprisoned and exiled for his faith. None of this dampened his spirits, but in typical fashion, Nicholas endured every hardship as a price to pay for the Gospel. His love of God far exceeded any earthly concerns.

Nicholas's reputation as a gift giver was never in doubt to those of his time, but one incident in particular has had a lasting impression on history. A local man had lost all he had, leaving him with no money to pay the dowry for his three daughters to marry. The man was in such desperate straits that he even considered selling one or more of his daughters to a brothel just to earn enough money to feed the rest of his family. He knew that without the dowry no man would marry his daughters.

The night before the desperate father was going to part with his oldest daughter, Nicholas went by the home. It was well after everyone was asleep. Knowing the man's situation, Nicholas tossed a small bag of gold through the window and continued on his way.

The next morning, the man awoke to find the bag of gold. It was enough money to pay the dowry for his daughter and care for his family for the next year.

When circumstances did not improve, the father was again faced with a daughter ready to marry, but without the required dowry. He was again faced with the prospect of sending his daughter to the brothel, when the strange visitor again went by the house in the dead of night, tossing a small bag of gold through the window. The man was again stunned when he awoke to find just what he and his family needed.

When the third daughter was ready to marry, the father stayed up to see if the benefactor would come again. He wanted to know who his anonymous benefactor was. He ran out of the house just after the small bag of gold landed on his floor, having arrived via the open window. He saw the Bishop's cloak and knew in an instant it was Nicholas. Although Nicholas responded to the man's heartfelt thanks by asking that he tell no one of the gift, the story has survived through the centuries, making Nicholas a patron saint for children and the ultimate giver of gifts.

Nicholas's generosity did not stop with giving gifts to children and needy families. On one occasion, three men were wrongly accused and sentenced to death. Nicholas went to the responsible officials and appealed for their release. He let it be known in no uncertain terms the grave sin about to be committed. His intervention swayed the officials and the men were released.

Nicholas was not hesitant to stand up for truth. In addition to his imprisonment, torture and exile under Diocletian, Nicholas boldly confronted the Arian heresy, a teaching by some that said Jesus was not God from the beginning, but was raised to "god status" given his sacrifice. Nicholas participated in the Council of Nicaea in 325, which resolved and condemned the heresy. Indeed, our profession of faith that we profess at Mass today comes from that very council, leaving no doubt that Jesus was and is "God from God, light from light, true God from True God" and a member of the Most Holy Trinity, yesterday, today, and forever. Indeed, at the council, Nicholas's zeal was so strong that he struck a proponent of Arius, the primary advocate of Christ being inferior to God the Father. As a result, he was precluded from wearing his Bishop's miter during the remainder of the council.

Nicholas did not die a martyr's death, but died peacefully in his old age on December 6, 343. He was venerated for living a life faithful to Jesus. He was beloved by sailors, who credit many miracles and their safety to his intercession. He is so revered that over 2,000 churches in Europe bear his name. As one anonymous Greek wrote in the 10th century, "The West as well as the East acclaims and glorifies him. Wherever there are people, in the country and the town, in the villages, in the isles, in the furthest parts of the earth, his name is revered and churches are built in his honor. Images of him are set up, panegyrics preached and festivals celebrated. All Christians, young and old, men and women, boys and girls, reverence his memory and call upon his protection. And his favors, which know no limit of time and continue from age to age, are poured out over all the earth; the Scythians know them, as do the Indians and the barbarians, the Africans as well as the Italians." When Vladimir I of Russia was baptized in Constantinople, he took the stories of Nicholas back to his native land. Saint Nicholas was quickly venerated throughout the country, being named as a patron saint of Russia, and remains in high esteem in the Russian Orthodox Church. When Columbus landed in Haiti, he named a port Saint Nicholas on December 6, 1492. Even the Spanish named an early Florida settlement Saint Nicholas Ferry in an area we now call Jacksonville.

When hostilities broke out near Myra in 1087, two Italian cities vied to be the new home for his remains. Ultimately Bari won out, and a cathedral was built in his honor to house his remains and the faithful continued to flock to the city to venerate his body.

The main reason for Saint Nicholas's veneration is not his selfless giving from his possessions or his fierce defense of the faith, but because he lived as Jesus calls all of us to live, by humbly following his Lord every day in every circumstance. When it would have been easier and safer to keep quiet, Saint Nicholas spoke up for the Truth and against injustice. When someone was in need, he could have stayed home or called on friends or associates to help, but instead, he got up in the middle of the night to give of his own treasure. For Nicholas, all he had was a gift from God, which was to be used in His service. That is how he lived his life and why he is the perfect symbol of Christmas, the perfect person to remind us what the gift of Christ's birth is all about.

We are all faced with challenges and opportunities in life. God will always give us chances to step up to the plate and serve Him with our time, our talent, and our treasure, indeed, our very lives. For Jesus said that whatever we do for the least of our brothers and sisters, we do for Him. During this Christmas season, as we prepare for the birth of Jesus, let us always remember that the greatest gift we can give is ourselves. For some, this means answering the call to the priesthood and religious life; Nicholas did. What a wonderful gift to give to the Lord. To find out what is being asked of us, we must Be Still … Be Not Afraid. To What is Jesus Calling You?

* * *

Saint Nicholas is a great example of what it means to model our faith in all we do. There is a time for patience, generosity, and gentleness, and a time for boldness, courage, and firmness. In all things, we should stand for and with Christ. We recall the simplicity and humility of Christ's birth. We recall the awe the shepherds felt at the angels' announcement and upon their arrival at the place where He lay. That scene compels us to give generously, as the men from the East did, and proclaim the Glory of God, as the angels did. Saint Nicholas lived the spirit of Christmas, the fundamental meaning and significance of Christ's birth, and we see that in all he did. Saint Nicholas set the example we are to follow by showing what it means to be a follower of Jesus.

Saint Nicholas's example goes beyond his generosity to a family in need. His steadfast defense of the faith in the face of a strong opposition should not be overlooked. He saw everything that he was called to be in following the Lord, in serving Him and the Church. As bishop, he had the responsibility to defend and preach the truth. He had to model the fullness of the faith. We are not fully Catholic or fully Christian if we only support part of the Church's mission or follow only part of Jesus' teaching. Social justice is an important part of the mission of the Church, but so is proclaiming the truth of who Jesus is. The Church proclaims the fullness of God's truth. Saint Nicholas understood that and stood for and lived the fullness of that truth. We are called to do the same, which may put us at odds with some who walk beside us in one aspect of fulfilling our baptismal call of following Jesus.

As in Saint Nicholas's time, our culture challenges the Gospel and suggests that self glorification is a virtue. We are challenged on the sacraments of marriage, the holiness of marital love, the sanctity of life from the moment of conception to natural death. We are told to do what is necessary to avoid consequences for our actions, and if no one gets hurt, (the stain of sin upon the soul and its effect on the whole community being ignored) then we should feel free to embrace it or at least not prohibit others from doing what they want. But secularism, materialism, humanism, and other similar philosophies deny the Truth of God's love, of why Jesus had to suffer and die and rise again, and what we are to be as followers of Jesus.

Saint Nicholas would have spoken out against the false teaching of culture and our Baptism calls on us to do the same, and stand up for the Truth. We overcome the misleading philosophies of modern culture by how we live, by standing in the light and defending the Gospel. If we do so, we will transform the world, which is what Jesus was born to do and what He calls us to do by faith. He asks us to bring His light to the world, and like Saint Nicholas, it will take the humility of faith and a staunch determination to stand up for Truth.

Living such a life may sound hard, but we must have faith that in standing up for Christ and promoting the Kingdom of God, our Lord will stand with us and the Truth will win out. It always has. Like the student in Tiananmen Square, we may be faced with staring down a seemingly immovable object, and that is not easy. It takes great courage and great faith to live out our baptismal call. Yet, that is the example of Saint Nicholas's life. It should also be the story of our own.

Chapter 15

GOD'S INTERACTION WITH man is not a thing of the past, but part of the present, part of God's relationship with man. At times, God uses Mary to help remind us of His great love and to again trumpet the call for repentance and conversion. The Blessed Mother has appeared countless places and always for a particular purpose. Her message is as it was at the wedding at Cana—do whatever Jesus tells us to do. She took the problems of the bride groom to the Lord and He solved them. As our mother, she calls to us, her children, to lead us to her Son. When she chooses a messenger, she often chooses among the meek and unassuming who ultimately prove to be the most faithful. This is so true of Saint Bernadette Soubirous.

SAINT BERNADETTE SOUBIROUS
(January 2009)

Throughout history, God has chosen the unassuming of the world to do great things for His kingdom. Many of those chosen are people we ourselves would never have selected for such important work. We even believe we are not worthy to be called in such a special way. One young, poor, and uneducated girl would be asked to take on a seemingly impossible task, yet her willingness to do just what God wanted of her resulted in more being accomplished than she could have ever imagined.

Bernadette Soubirous was born to Louise and Francois Soubirous on January 7, 1844, in Lourdes, France. Life for Bernadette was not easy. Her parents owned a mill, which should have brought a good living for her family, but her father was not much of a businessman. Her mother loved to entertain and provide free samples of the bread, cheese and wine. With her mother fond of the wine and her father fond of the café, it was only a matter of time before the family of six, two girls and two younger boys, lost their mill, an eventuality that came to pass in 1854.

The family spent the next two years going from place to place, relocating each time they were unable to pay the rent. Finding no other place to go, the family moved in with a cousin of her mother's in what used to be a prison. The home was a single room of about eight feet by ten feet. There was a small space for a kitchen and fireplace. The family put in two small beds. No one else was willing to live in the room Bernadette's family called home.

In March 1857, Bernadette's father was accused of stealing flour from a man for whom he made deliveries. Although he was never convicted, the family's standing in the community was at its lowest possible point.

With no money and little food, Bernadette was sent to live with a woman who acted as a foster mother to her and needed help tending the lambs on her farm. The woman promised to teach Bernadette her catechism, but she found teaching the young girl so difficult that she gave up. With the work at the house, Bernadette did not make it to school very often, either. After three months, Bernadette finally convinced her parents to let her come home.

Bernadette could not read and given that she grew up speaking a local dialect and not French, she found school to be very difficult. Her family was constantly on the verge of starvation, scavenging for bits of wood and bone to sell just to buy enough bread to eat. Through it all, her family loved each other and stuck together.

Returning home in January 1858, Bernadette began taking classes to make her First Holy Communion. She knew the Lord's Prayer and would pray, but she knew little else. So here she was, a girl of 14, with dark hair and steady eyes, who was from a family few would associate with and a future as uncertain as any could be. But life for her, Lourdes, and the world was about to change.

On Thursday, February 11, 1858, the weather was wet and cold. Bernadette, who went without breakfast for there was no wood for cooking the food, asked to go with her younger sister and a friend to see if they could find any wood. Her mother relented and the girls set off for the river, Gave de Pau, which ran through town.

Upon arriving at the river bank, the girls had to cross a small stream to get back on the mainland under an outcropping of rock known as Massabielle. This was an area where local pig farmers used to let the swine hunt for food. Bernadette, who had had a constant cough since she was six years old, did not want to get her feet wet. Her sister and friend took off their shoes, stockings, hiked up their skirts and walked on through the cold water. When Bernadette asked them to carry her or put stones in the water so she could walk across, they said she should cross just as they had.

As the girls walked off, Bernadette looked for a way to cross. She then heard a rustling of wind, but none of the trees were moving. She noticed an old wild rose bush in a niche in the rock across the stream; it was moving. She was drawn to it and crossed the water. When her sister and friend turned to look for her, they saw Bernadette kneeling down praying her Rosary, but nothing else. It was not until they were on their way home that Bernadette told her sister that she saw a young lady, no bigger than she was, dressed in white with a blue sash and a yellow rose on each foot. The lady did not say anything, but she carried a rosary of white beads and a gold chain.

The next three weeks would be trying times and wonderful times for Bernadette. News of the vision spread, with many, given her family's reputation, believing it was either a hoax or a hallucination. Others, however, believed something incredible might have happened. Her parents fluctuated from allowing her to return to the grotto to forbidding her from visiting there. Over the next week, Bernadette, at the urging of friends and neighbors, tested her lady by throwing holy water on her and giving her a pen, ink, and paper to write down what she wanted.

When the lady finally spoke, she asked Bernadette to return to the grotto for 15 days. The town and surrounding area became a buzz with believers and cynics alike. The priests were forbidden from attending. The police investigated to determine if her claim was a hoax for getting people to give the poor family money. Bernadette was called in for questioning by the chief prosecutor and inspector, but her story, humble and simple as it was, never wavered. The number of people who gathered at the grotto for the apparitions grew from just a few to several thousand.

People were captivated when they saw Bernadette's face during the apparition. They described her as looking like an angel when she spoke to her lady. When the lady asked Bernadette to pray for sinners, and had her walk on her knees up and down the rocky slope of the grotto, many thought she was mad. On February 25, Bernadette was asked to drink and wash in the spring. She immediately turned to walk to the river, but was called back toward the cave. The lady pointed to a spot where there was just a trickle of water. Bernadette scratched at the ground and tried to scoop up what appeared to be nothing more than muddy water. Finally, she was able to drink a sip and then obediently ate the green plant found growing at that spot.

Bernadette was given three secrets, but they were things she was to never reveal and she remained true to her word. She was also given a message for the priests. The lady wanted a procession and a chapel built at the grotto. The local pastor, a great skeptic of the apparitions, told Bernadette that her lady needed to tell him her name and make the old rose bush bloom.

On March 4th, the 15 days ended before 20,000 people, but without a great sign, just the saying of the rosary three times and Bernadette leaving in silence. Even with this apparent disappointment, people began to venerate the young 14-year-old as a saint, something that made her very uncomfortable.

People began turning the grotto into a chapel with candles, a crucifix, and even a sanctuary light. On March 25th, the Feast of the Annunciation, Bernadette returned to the grotto where the lady finally confirmed her identity with these words, "I am the Immaculate Conception. I want a chapel built here." The local pastor remained incredulous at this revelation, but it is supposed that he could not fight the truth of what the young girl had seen. After all, Bernadette had no way of knowing what Our Lady's declaration meant, but the priest sure did.

The grotto became a sight for impersonators and false visionaries. It was closed to the public, but people still went there for the water and to pray. Even with so many flocking to the spot, it was Bernadette's witness, often given at the request of her family, and later the sisters who took her in, that changed most people's hearts and minds. The local bishop came to meet with her, and at the conclusion of her story, he not only believed, but he wept. On January 18, 1862, four years after the apparitions had begun, the local bishop officially declared that the Blessed Mother had indeed appeared to Bernadette Soubirous at Lourdes.

Bernadette lived at home for two years following the apparitions before moving into the local hospice. She was often ill, but helped out where she could, in the kitchens, the workroom, and the infirmary.

Bernadette wanted to leave the chaos behind and live in seclusion. The Bishop gave his approval for her to enter the convent of the Sisters of Nevers in 1863, over the objection of the Mother Superior, who felt Bernadette did not have skills that would assist them. Her frequent illness, however, prevented her from traveling until 1866.

At Nevers, Bernadette was belittled by some of her superiors, but she bore it all with humility. She was called on to tell her story to the new postulants, who were then told they were not to speak of it again. Bernadette befriended some younger sisters to help them through the often difficult transition to religious life. She was known for her simplicity and humility. She continued to live as she always had, trying to do what was asked of her and drawing no attention to herself. Bernadette likened herself to a broom that should be put in the corner after it had served its purpose. After all, she only did what Our Lady asked of her. She died far too young on April 16, 1879, at the age of 35.

Our Lady got her chapel in April 1866 when the crypt was opened. A larger, and the second of three churches now in Lourdes, was opened in 1870. Millions of pilgrims travel to Lourdes with countless claims of spiritual and physical healing attributed to the water Mary pointed out to Bernadette. In the end, the response to Our Lady's message was far greater than Bernadette could have ever imagined.

Bernadette always knew when Mary was ready to speak to her by the yearning in her heart to go to the Grotto. When things looked too difficult or she did not understand what was being asked of her, she remained faithful and carried out Mary's wishes by telling only what she had been asked to tell. In the end, millions have had their faith in God restored due to what happened in Lourdes during that spring of 1858.

We too need to realize that we are called to carry out the plans God has for us. The peer pressure may become strong, and doing God's work may seem too difficult. This can be especially true today when answering a call to the priesthood or religious life. In the end, however, we are only called to do what God asks of us, and like Bernadette, He will give us the strength, smarts, and words to accomplish all He has in store for us. If we do, the joy Bernadette experienced when visited by Our Lady will be the same joy we experience as we continue to build God's kingdom here on earth. So, Be Still … Be Not Afraid. To What is Jesus Calling You?

* * *

The appearance of the Blessed Mother at Lourdes has been written about, talked about, and made into a movie. Our Lady's words to Bernadette were for prayer for sinners, repentance, and conversion. Sin takes us away from God; it erects a barrier that keeps us from His grace. God gives us what we need to bring down those barriers and conquer sin. Jesus' life, passion, death, and resurrection destroyed the power of sin and death. Bernadette was not a likely candidate to share that message with anyone, let alone the world, but by humbly doing what Mary asked of her, she did just that. So many were caught up in the miracles that they missed the meaning of what happened.

We are each called by God to hear His voice and answer His call. Bernadette did so in spite of great opposition from family, friends, townspeople, her pastor, and even the local police who accused her of being a charlatan. But Bernadette kept her focus on Mary and did exactly as she was told, and the blessings that flowed from her obedience not only brought joy to Bernadette, but brought peace, joy, and healing to millions. Our Lady's call was fulfilled, for many repented and converted their lives back to God. If we spread the seeds God gives us, we too will help produce a great harvest.

The miracles of Lourdes are many. Some point to the miraculous healings as proof of the authenticity of Saint Bernadette's visions. The countless number of people healed by the water of Lourdes makes it impossible to deny that something special, something beyond our understanding, happened. But the outward signs are not what Our Lady came for. She did not appear flashy or give in to the local priest's demand for a sign. Our Lady responded just as her Son did when the people demanded a sign—we have already been given all the signs we need with the prophets and the Resurrection. What is needed is faith and obedience and the miraculous signs will naturally appear.

The skeptic who does not believe God works miracles continues to test the Lord. Saint Bernadette would not test Our Lady by demanding a sign before doing what was asked of her. The fruits of Our Lady's appearance—prayer, peace, joy—told Saint Bernadette all she needed to know. Saint Bernadette knew she was not called to perform miracles—she never healed anyone during her lifetime—but to do what Mary asked of her. When she did, she discovered Jesus. That is the sign that converted millions.

Chapter 16

JULY 2008 TO June 2009 was the Year of Saint Paul. We recalled his conversion, his faith, and his mission to the Gentiles. Saint Paul's place within the Church cannot be overstated and most of the New Testament after the Gospels was written by Saint Paul and contains his teaching, his encouragement, and his chastisement of those who went astray. There is much to learn from Saint Paul's letters and from looking at how God worked in his life.

SAINT PAUL
(March 2009)

In the *Book of Revelation*, John writes that the Lord told him to write to the church in Laodicea, "I know what you have done; I know that you are neither cold nor hot. How I wish you were either one or the other! But because you are lukewarm, neither hot nor cold, I am going to spit you out of my mouth!" If there was ever someone who was never lukewarm, it was Saint Paul. His life is defined by his passion and zeal. He was not one who sat on the fence.

Saint Paul was born about ten years after Jesus, in the city of Tarsus. Paul was "of the tribe of Benjamin, a Hebrew of Hebrew parentage, [and] in observance of the law a Pharisee." His family was originally from Galilee, but was likely moved to Tarsus by the Romans after an uprising in the area

before Paul was born. It is believed his family was sold as slaves to a
Roman family in Tarsus, and gained Roman citizenship when they were
freed.

Tarsus was a cosmopolitan city with a strong Greek influence. It is lo-
cated in modern day Turkey about ten miles from the River Cydnus. The
city was a popular and important city on the trade routes from east to west,
which meant there was a lot of business coming through the city. Paul's
family was well off because with so much market space being rented to
merchants, his family, who made tents, always had customers for their
services.

In Tarsus, Jews were a noted minority in a city dominated by Gentiles
and Greeks. Most in the city were pagans, as that was the dominant religion
of the Roman Empire. Still, Paul grew up devoted to his heritage. He
learned the Scriptures and was devoted to following the Law. So, growing
up in a city whose major festival honored a pagan god, for Paul to keep the
Law of Moses means he was quite devout.

Paul was well educated not only in the Scriptures, but in Greek philosophy and the art of rhetoric. Greek philosophy held that there was some
level of divine reason in man, that one was responsible for one's choices,
and that all things happen for a reason. As such, he was not to complain
about the bad, such as pain or sickness, any more than he was to take pride
in the good, such as wealth or fame. His training would serve him well
when he began his missionary work.

Paul departed for Jerusalem, a journey of over 500 miles, when he was
around 20 years old. He would make his way to the Temple, the center of
spiritual life for him as a Jew. He was most likely overwhelmed when he
first saw the Temple. It dominated the city. He would have had to find an
introduction to those in authority and find a place to live. Paul's family's
status and wealth undoubtedly assisted him in both tasks.

We know from Paul's own writings that he ultimately studied under
Gamaliel, the most influential Pharisee of his time. The Pharisees did not
have power in the Temple, but did have seats on the Sanhedrin, and
Gamaliel served as a check on the High Priest, Caiaphas. The dynamics of
political and spiritual life in Jerusalem at the time were such that Paul would
learn a lot by observing these two powerful men.

Paul never met Jesus, but he surely heard of him. While Paul does not appear in the Gospels during this time, no doubt due to his age and inexperience, he was certainly aware of the discussions regarding Jesus, and the plot to arrest him, given that he sat at the feet of Gamaliel.

As a Pharisee, Paul was zealous in his observance of the law and devoted to his ancestral traditions. When someone challenged the law or attempted to diminish the importance of the Temple, Paul would become as angry as anyone. As a result, Paul was most likely troubled by Jesus' following. This may also explain why he later split with Gamaliel and helped the Sanhedrin persecute the early Church.

The breaking point with Gamaliel most likely came when Peter and the other apostles were brought before the Council to answer for preaching in the name of Jesus. The High Priest and the Council wanted the apostles put to death, but it was Gamaliel who stayed their hand. He convinced them that the apostles were of no danger and warned the Council that if what the apostles preached was from God, then the Council could not oppose them, and if what they preached was from man, then it would die out on its own. Given his stature, the Council agreed, but Paul was most likely taken aback. The apostles were teaching not only that the chief priests were responsible for Jesus' death, but that Jesus had been raised from the dead and was actually the Son of God.

Still, the Sadducees and Paul could not just ignore the Apostles and so they turned their focus to Saint Stephen. When questioned, Stephen spoke boldly against the chief priests and elders, which angered them so much they threw him out and stoned him. It is here that Paul first appears in Scripture as the one who held the cloaks of those who murdered Saint Stephen, an act of which we are told Paul approved.

Paul then carried on the work of the Sanhedrin against the early church, going house to house to imprison those who professed Jesus as Lord. He took his new found responsibility seriously and carried it out with much vigor. He was on his way to Damascus to destroy the church there when his life took a dramatic turn.

The story of Paul's conversion is probably the most well known conversion story in history. On the road to Damascus, with a mission to arrest those who taught or professed Jesus as the Christ, Paul was knocked to the ground. He was surrounded by a blinding light, and none of his companions could see what was happening, but they could hear what happened next.

Paul heard a voice say, "Saul, Saul, why are you persecuting me?" In response, Paul said, "Who are you, sir?" Paul then got his answer, "I am Jesus whom you persecute. Now get up and go into the city and you will be told what you must do." When Jesus left him, Paul was completely blind. His companions then took him inside the city.

Paul fasted and prayed. Then the Lord appeared to a disciple named Ananias and asked him to go to Paul and lay hands on him so that he may regain his sight. Ananias knew of Paul and protested because of all the evil Paul had done against the Church. But the Lord told him that Paul "is a chosen instrument of mine to carry my name before Gentiles, kings, and Israelites." So Ananias did just as he was told.

At Paul's conversion, the Lord revealed to Paul what he would have to suffer for Christ's sake. As Paul would later tell us, he suffered plenty. As he put it: "Five times I was given the 39 lashes by the Jews; three times I was whipped by the Romans; and once I was stoned. I have been in three shipwrecks, and once I spent 24 hours in the water. In my many travels, I have been in danger from floods and from robbers, in danger from fellow Jews and from Gentiles; there have been dangers in the cities, dangers in the wilds, dangers on the high seas, and dangers from false friends. There has been work and toil; often I have gone without sleep; I have been hungry and thirsty; I have often been without enough food, shelter, or clothing. And not to mention other things, every day I am under the pressure of my concern for all the churches. ... When I was in Damascus, the governor under King Aretas placed guards at the city gates to arrest me. But I was let down in a basket through an opening in the wall and escaped from him." Paul was bitten by a snake, abandoned by his friends, and ultimately beheaded in Rome.

Even knowing a small portion of this, most would say "no thanks," but not Paul. Jesus was the promised Messiah and Paul would accept every hardship as God's will. Paul would do everything he could to bring as many people as possible to Jesus.

There are three aspects to Paul's ministry worth noting. The first is that he knew it was important to learn from Peter. Three years after his conversion, Paul spent two weeks with Peter in Jerusalem learning all that Jesus taught and did. Hearing the Gospel directly from those who lived with Jesus was critical to Paul's ministry. He also understood how important it was to work within the Church and that he was not to be apart from it.

The second aspect to Paul's ministry is the overriding theme of love. Paul's conversion was so powerful because he realized that Jesus, who was without sin and did not need to die, chose out of love to lay down his life for all of us. Paul's letters are filled with exhortations of the importance of loving one another. He admonishes his readers that no matter what good they do, if they do not have love then none of it matters. While he is often looked upon as the one who sets down hard and fast rules, such a view misses his central theme which is Christ's command that we love one another.

The third aspect to Paul's ministry is his emphasis on conversion and repentance. No one should ever believe that God cannot forgive them after reading Paul's letters. Indeed, Paul considered himself the poster boy for God's great love and mercy. To Timothy, Paul wrote: "By calling me into service he has judged me trustworthy, even though I used to be a blasphemer and a persecutor and contemptuous. Mercy, however, was shown me, because while I lacked faith I acted in ignorance; but the grace of our Lord filled me with faith and with the love that is in Christ Jesus. Here is a saying that you can rely on and nobody should doubt: that Christ Jesus came into the world to save sinners. I myself am the greatest of them; and if mercy has been shown to me, it is because Jesus Christ meant to make me the leading example of his inexhaustible patience for all the other people who were later to trust in him for eternal life." So from Paul, we should never feel that God will not accept us or use us for something great. He will.

This is the year of Saint Paul. It is a good time to revisit his devotion, his passion for Jesus and make it our own. For Paul, he chose to follow Christ as his priest and apostle to the Gentiles. Today, too many think religious life is too difficult, too much of a sacrifice. But as Saint Paul came to realize, a life in service of Jesus and His Church is but a small price to pay for what Jesus gave up for us. Jesus told Paul what he wanted of him, and

Paul said yes. For us, to hear what is being asked of us, we must Be Still …
Be Not Afraid, To What is Jesus Calling You?

* * *

God calls all of us. For some, He knocks you off your high horse, like Paul,
while for others, He whispers in the silence when we are still. It is important to be aware of when God is calling and what He is asking of us.
Some may try to see a sign in just about everything, while others will ignore
even the most obvious of calls. From Paul, we should know that none of us
are worthy, but all of us are called, because by God's grace we can all be
saints. The Lord gives us all unique gifts and calls us to use them in support
of the Church's mission of spreading the Gospel. As Saint Paul said, all of
us have different gifts and all have a part to play but not all are called or
meant to be Pope.

We serve Jesus as He calls us. Jesus called Paul for a daunting mission
of spreading the Gospel among the Gentiles, while other saints were called
for different roles. Saint Therese was called to do little acts of love and pray
in the silence of Mount Carmel for the conversion of sinners and for
priests, while Saint Bernadette was called to pass along Mary's request for a
church, and Saint Maximilian Kolbe was called to spread the faith by print
and offer his life to save another in the hell of Auschwitz. As Mother
Teresa told us, we are not called to be "successful," but to be faithful and as
Pope John Paul II said, we should be proud of the Gospel. When we answer God's call in our lives that is precisely what we do.

Before his conversion, Saint Paul was so headstrong in defending "the
Law" that he forgot that he was actually called to live and defend the Faith.
Our lives are to be in accordance with God's call in our lives, and that is
where we find the most amazing blessings. Our path is the one God sets
out for us, not just any old path of doing good, but one where our gifts and
talents are used to bring about the Kingdom of God. So how we live our
lives must be in answer to God's call, and they must be lived according to
that great virtue of love that Saint Paul spoke so beautifully about in his
letter to the Corinthians. How we work, how we treat our spouse and our
children, how we treat friends and strangers alike, and how we spend our

time should all be a reflection of Christ's love. Saint Paul preached so that everyone might come to know Jesus and believe in Him. We are called to live so that all we meet will experience Jesus in us.

The faith spread because Saint Paul followed Christ and put aside his doubts and fears to accept the Truth. Our lives must likewise bear witness to the Truth. God will give us all we need to do just that. We just have to follow Him.

Chapter 17

TO PREACH TO people who do not know Christ as Saint Paul did is not easy. To minister to those with an illness that is fatal and highly contagious is another level of faith that few have, and few are called to make that sacrifice. Father Damian answered that call and fulfilled his ministry with such joy and humility that we all can learn a great lesson from him when facing the challenges in our lives.

SAINT DAMIEN
(May 2009)

In the fifth chapter of Luke's Gospel we read about Jesus healing a man "full of leprosy." At the man's plea to be made clean, Jesus reaches out and does the unthinkable, he touches him. Leprosy is an awful, incurable, and deadly disease, and in Jesus' time, and for the next 1,900 years, those who had it were exiled and segregated from the rest of the community. Compassion was from a distance, but for one man, his life's vocation was to provide comfort for the poor lepers in Hawaii.

Joseph De Veuster was born January 3, 1840, in Tremelo, Belgium. He was the seventh of eight children. His father tended to the family farm, while his mother cared for the children. She was the source of faith in the family, as well. The family had a book on the lives of the saints and the kids would often ask their mother to read about the hermits and those who left the world behind to serve Jesus and the Church.

Three of Joseph's older siblings entered religious life, two sisters and one brother. However, Joseph, a strong, broad-shouldered boy, was seen as destined for the farm. He was taken out of school at the age of 13 to learn the work on the farm.

Joseph was known for his kindness to those in need, whether it was helping with a sick cow or giving his lunch to someone claiming to be without food. Still, Joseph yearned for more than the farm. At age 18, Joseph returned to school for the purpose of preparing himself for the grain trade. But regardless of his parents' intention, Joseph concluded he had a vocation and it was "his turn" to join his brother and sisters in religious life. His Christmas 1858 letter home was clear: Do not stop me, he wrote, "because to forbid your son to follow the will of God in choosing a condition of life would be an ingratitude that would bring down cruel punishments on you. Are you not afraid of making an irreparable mistake if I lose a vocation for which God has destined me since my childhood, which would make me unhappy forever? Because, you know, the choice of a life to which God calls us decides our happiness after this life. So my vocation has nothing in it to make you sad."

Joseph was very close to his elder brother, Auguste. His brother had entered the Congregation of the Sacred Hearts of Jesus and Mary, taking the name Pamphile. He convinced Joseph that he should join his order over others Joseph was considering. With such an invitation, he could not refuse.

Joseph spoke Flemish, and his ability to get along in French, the language of the Congregation, was limited. He also had no knowledge of Latin or Greek, so he was not considered to be a very good candidate for the priesthood. Still, Joseph was pleased to accept a religious vocation that did not include being a priest right away.

What Joseph wanted was to become a missionary. He prayed to Saint Francis Xavier, the missionary to the East. At the age of 20, when he took his vows of chastity, poverty, and obedience on October 7, 1860, he took the name of Damien, an ancient physician. Damien's ceremony left a lasting impression on him in more ways than the taking of his vows. The ceremony followed a funeral rite, with candlelight, incense, and he was covered with a funeral pall while lying prostrate before the altar. When he rose, his old self had died, and he had risen anew as a religious. He was no longer Joseph, but Damien, and his life belonged to Christ.

In 1863, the congregation was going to send additional missionaries to the Hawaiian Islands. The congregation had been sending missionaries to the islands for 35 years and new missionaries were needed, especially priests. Damien's brother, Pamphile, was selected to go, while Damien was asked to stay behind. When there was an outbreak of typhus in the area, Pamphile caught the disease while visiting the sick, so he was unable to make the journey. Damien wrote to the Father General of the Order asking to take his brother's place, and his request was granted. He departed on October 3, 1863.

Damien was still young, inexperienced, and had not completed his studies for the priesthood, something he did not do until March 19, 1864, two months after his arrival in Hawaii. Damien's dream of being a missionary was realized, but he could not have known what that life would be like.

The Hawaiian culture was very different than that of Europe, particularly when it came to social morals. The people were known to be very permissive and promiscuous. Damien wrote home, "Here I am a priest, dear parents, here I am a missionary in a corrupt, heretical, idolatrous country." He asked for their prayers.

Damien was assigned to an expansive area of one of the islands. By foot and horseback and sometimes canoe, he traveled over rough terrain and sea to visit his flock of about 350 families. He built homes and churches, raised pigs, and grew his own food. Most important to Damien was administering the sacraments, especially Baptism, Eucharist, and Confession.

Damien was successful in his ministry because he would sit with people where they were, while others would not even share a meal with the local population. Damien was not a great preacher, but he cared for people and had a great concern for their souls. Damien was very passionate about the Truth of his faith. For the locals, his actions spoke louder than his words.

In 1866, in an effort to stem the tide of a leprosy epidemic, the Hawaiian Kingdom instituted a segregation policy isolating all those found with the disease, many being sent to a small village on the island of Molokai. If there was a hell on earth, it was on Molokai. The village of Kalawao was on a peninsula surrounded on three sides by a steep climb to a plateau and on the other rough seas with no port. It was as isolated as a village could be. If the leper settlement were not there, it would have been considered a paradise, but as it were, this piece of land was no Eden.

The situation there was horrible. Lawlessness ruled the day as the people condemned to life on Molokai knew that death was their only way off the island. There was rampant drunkenness, prostitution, hording and stealing of food, and other behaviors that only increased the suffering of those on the island.

In 1873, there was a call for someone to step in and help the poor inhabitants in the village of Kalawao on Molokai. There were several hundred Catholics in the village of 800 souls, and rarely did a priest make it to minister to their needs. The Bishop was not willing to simply assign a priest to the village, so, while Damien and others were in Honolulu, the Bishop asked if anyone was willing to serve the people condemned to the island. Damien and three other priests volunteered. The idea was that each would serve three months at a time, but Damien would get it started. In the end, Damien was permitted to stay for as long as he wanted, which turned out to be for the rest of his life.

At the age of 33, Damien stepped off the boat with only his breviary for his daily prayers. The settlement had a small church dedicated to Saint Philomena, but there was no house for Damien. He spent the next several weeks laying his head upon a rock beneath a tree until he built himself a home. He was warned to not touch anyone for fear of catching the highly contagious disease. Doctors who were on the island before would not touch the people; one would lift the bandages with his cane while another would leave medicine on a table for the patient to take. The inhabitants were separated from friends and family, and this was not a place people could or would visit, so touch was important.

The scene of people whose flesh was eaten away, fingers and toes lost, faces unrecognizable, must have been overwhelming. The smell was of death. Damien wrote shortly after his arrival on how he came to cope with the suffering and squalor he found: "Many a time in fulfilling my priestly duties at the lepers' homes, I have been obliged, not only to close my nostrils, but to remain outside to breathe fresh air. To counteract the bad smell, I got myself accustomed to the use of tobacco. The smell of the pipe preserved me somewhat from carrying in my clothes the obnoxious odor of our lepers."

Damien again found a way to put himself in the community with the people. At Mass, he referred to "we lepers." He soon gave up on the idea of not touching the people, and began bandaging their wounds, anointing their heads with oil, and placing the Eucharist on tongues in mere remnants of mouths. He rebuilt the church and put a fence around the cemetery to keep the pigs and dogs out. He visited everyone at least once a week.

Damien knew he could not cure the body, but he would cure the soul. He did more than speak out about the drunkenness and sexual immorality taking place. He went into the house used for such gatherings and with his walking stick broke up the party. He let people know that they retained their dignity, so they should act like it. Death was a certainty, so they needed to be prepared for life in heaven.

Over the next 16 years, the dilapidated grass huts were replaced by small homes, many built by Damien. An orphanage was built for all the children sentenced to the island. Damien developed a funeral committee so that everyone who died received a proper funeral and burial. He built many of the coffins. He developed a choir, often with people playing instruments together so they could find ten fingers between the two of them. People learned to grow and raise food, the children played games. Damien even instituted perpetual adoration in Kalawao.

Damien's life was certainly not easy. But his greatest suffering was being without a religious companion for confession and conversation. On one occasion, because the Bishop was not allowed on the island and Damien was not allowed to leave, Damien met the Bishop's boat at sea just off the island. The captain would not allow Damien on board, so he shouted his confession to the Bishop as the other passengers looked on.

All during this time, Damien knew he was flirting with death. His health remained remarkably strong for 12 years. These 12 years were in answer to his prayer before he ever left for Hawaii, when he prayed to Our Lady of Montaigu for the privilege of 12 years in the missionary vineyard.

He got 12 years on Molokai before, in early 1885, Damien was diagnosed with leprosy.

It began with the loss of feeling in his left foot, which he noticed when he scalded the foot and felt no pain. Later, the skin spots started to show on his face. Damien continued to work as hard as his body would allow while he battled the disease. He was told to not leave the island, even to have his confession heard. Ultimately, a group of sisters came to the island to assist, a layman from the United States also joined Father Damien and was a tremendous help to him, and in 1888, Father Damien finally had a priest join him from whom he could get regular spiritual direction and receive reconciliation.

Father Damien died among his lepers on April 15, 1889, the day after Palm Sunday. He was buried in the cemetery outside of Saint Philomena's. His life was spent loving and caring for all God's children. The Holy Spirit did not abandon the people on Molokai. In the midst of the most extreme suffering, Damien helped them discover hope and joy. There was light in the darkness. The love of Jesus was real, the people just had to accept it and these people, who had no reason to see hope or to see a bright side to a most dreadful situation, found just that because Damien cared that much.

Father Damien's life also tells us how important it is to pray for our priests. They are all common kids from common families doing extraordinary work. Some, like Damien, are left without regular contact with their fellow religious, but they persevere. Damien knew that for him to serve God, he needed to receive the sacraments just as the people on Molokai needed the sacraments. As Damien's parents gave their blessing to Damien's call, we must be willing to give our blessing and encouragement to our children as they contemplate a religious vocation.

Jesus reached out his hand to touch the leper and healed him. Father Damien shared the love of Jesus with the leper, and they were healed in spirit. Father Damien may have died a leper's death, but he lived a holy life. In the midst of the greatest of despair and suffering, he found and shared hope, joy, and peace. He found his hope, his joy, his peace by listening to God's call and answering it. For us to find true joy and peace, we must answer God's call, we must Be Still ... Be Not Afraid, To What is Jesus Calling You?

* * *

Saint Damien defines heroism, but if you were to ask him, he would probably tell you he was only doing what God called him to do. Saint Damien
stood up for the dignity of the people condemned to Molakai. He fought
for what was right and dedicated his life to serving those whom no one else
would serve. There are many people in every community who demonstrate
such heroism. The common thread is that these heroes love what they do,
they love bringing joy to others, they love doing, modeling, and teaching
what is right.

Saint Damien knew we are all called to follow Christ and obey his
commandments. No circumstance, even the circumstance that brought the
residents of Molokai to that isolated place, justified one to not live a holy
life. Saint Damien did not pity his flock, he loved them and demanded of
them the dignity God gave them. Sin destroys the soul, which makes it
more deadly than any disease that destroys or kills the body. He taught his
flock that even with a dreadful and deadly disease, we must nourish our
souls and live the life God called us to live. Sacraments are key to the health
of the soul. We need to remember that.

From Saint Damien, we learn there is never a reason to despair. We
belong to God and as a result, at all times and in all circumstances, we must
live as children of God. Culture would say, "Look, they are dying so why
worry about prostitution or drunkenness. It helps them cope and brings a
little happiness." Such false teaching ignores God's love and God's
commandments.

Life does not end with death, for death just begins our time in eternity.
Saint Damien knew that with despair came a rejection of God's love, of the
promise He made to be with us always, even in the darkest hours of life.
Indeed, for the people on Molokai and people everywhere who struggle and
hurt, truly dreadful conditions are not an excuse to turn away from God's
commandments, but a reminder to place all our sufferings, pain, and sad-
ness in His hands. When the people of Molokai did just that, they found joy
in the midst of despair and hope in the midst of hopelessness. In each other
and in the sacraments, they discovered that not only had God not

abandoned them, but there He was in their midst, just like He is for us in the dark valleys of our life.

Chapter 18

AS DISCIPLES OF Christ, we are called to obedience. But, it is difficult to accept a difficult assignment, particularly one that is unjust, out of simple obedience. The idea that someone can give us a direction and we are obligated to follow, without question, is foreign to so many of us. Saint Damien, however, continued to serve the people of Molokai out of joyful obedience to his bishop and his prayer for missionary work. Padre Pio accepted isolation and the unjust loss of sacramental privileges without a word of protest. Their quiet suffering and joyful obedience speaks volumes to their faith and the faith we are called to have in Christ Jesus. It is difficult to think we are not the ones who get to make all the decisions in our lives or establish all the rules, but we are not called to do that. We are called to be faithful followers of Jesus. We are called to remain faithful to the teachings of the Church, even if we disagree or do not understand why the Church teaches what she does. That is part of the call of being Christian. The graces that flow from such obedience, even in the face of seemingly unjust decrees, are most evident in the life of Saint Padre Pio. He suffered quietly and obediently to bring glory to God and to bring thousands to Christ.

SAINT PIO OF PIETRELCINA
(November 2009)

If I were to describe to you someone who could be in two places at the same time, tell you about relatives half a world away, tell you everything you had ever done, heal the sick, conversed with Jesus, Mary, and his guardian angel, and was attacked by demons, you would probably assume I was describing a character out of Harry Potter. Such supernatural phenomena are relegated to fantasy, not the real world, or so we are led to believe. Yet, God still works in mysterious ways and he did so in the life of Saint Padre Pio of Pietrelcina.

Born Francesco Forgione on May 25, 1887, the future Padre Pio was the fourth child born to Grazio Forgione and Giuseppa De Nunzio. Three of his siblings died in infancy, including an older brother who was also named Francesco. His parents ran a small farm and instilled in their children a love of God, Mary, and the Church. Francesco had three years of schooling, the first of which was from a 14-year-old boy, which was all anyone received because children were needed to help with farm work. Most of the families in Pietrelcina owned little to nothing.

Francesco was a normal but conscientious boy. He played jokes, had friends, but did not like it when they cursed. At the age of ten, Francesco was intrigued by a young Capuchin friar who went from town to town to obtain provisions for his monastery 13 miles away. The friar was good with kids and a good preacher. Francesco told his parents he wanted to become a friar. When they suggested he consider becoming a parish priest, he said no, he wanted to be a friar with a beard.

His parents supported his youthful curiosity and took him to meet the friar at the monastery. While the Capuchin lifestyle was austere and held strictly to the Rule of Saint Francis, Francesco was certain that was what he wanted. If he was going to be a priest, however, he needed more education. His parents did not have the money for a private school, so his father traveled to America to work and sent money home so the young boy could get the education he needed.

When it came time to enter the monastery, Francesco almost got cold feet. He fretted leaving his family, but a local priest reassured him. In 1903, Francesco entered the Capuchin Order with his mother entrusting him to the care of Saint Francis.

Life in the monastery was far from luxurious. He had a mattress filled with corn husks, which was supported by four wooden posts, a little table, chair, wash stand, jug of water, and a wooden cross on the wall. After 16 days, he was stripped of his jacket and given the habit of Saint Francis. Francesco took the name Pio, most likely after Saint Pius.

The novitiate was hard and the novice master can only be described as cruel, yet Friar Pio did not complain. He prayed and studied a lot while eating modest food with little recreation.

As Friar Pio was getting close to finishing his studies for the priest-hood, he was stricken with a serious and unexplained illness. He was bed-ridden and unable to eat. Several times it was thought he would not survive. Given his condition, he was permitted to temporarily leave the monastery and live at home in Pietrelcina. It was there that he would finish his studies, and on August 10, 1910, he was ordained a priest. His hometown loved the young priest and wanted to keep him, but Padre Pio wanted to please his superiors and complete the vocation to which he had been called. His continuing illness created stress between him and his spiritual director who wanted him back in the monastery.

During this time, Padre Pio offered himself as a victim for the conversion of souls and the souls in purgatory. God granted his prayer and on September 7, 1910, wounds appeared on his hands, feet and side. While Padre Pio was happy to suffer pain to save sinners, he did not want the outward sign, which caused him much embarrassment. He and a friend prayed that God would take the visible wounds away and let him suffer in private, and again, God answered his prayer.

For nearly seven years, Padre Pio was back and forth between home and a monastery, never able to make it more than a couple of days before falling deathly ill. Still, his reputation grew, and in 1915, he began to provide spiritual direction to others. This proved to be the impetus to get him back to the monastery the following year when he went to visit a spiritual daughter who had fallen ill. At that time, Padre Pio was ordered to remain at the monastery in Foggia. As before, however, he again became quite ill. That summer he visited a monastery in the hills of San Giovanni Rotondo, a home to seven friars and a place that would ultimately become his home for the next 52 years.

In 1917, Padre Pio was finally granted permission to hear confessions. That same year, he was drafted into the Italian Army for service during the First World War, service he ultimately avoided due to his health.

While already gaining a reputation for extraordinary spirituality and supernatural phenomena, Padre Pio's life would change forever on September 20, 1918. While praying in the choir loft, Padre Pio had a vision of the crucified Christ. During the vision, Padre Pio was pierced on his hands, feet and side. This time, the visible stigmata would remain with him for 50 years.

The stigmata are not common signs. It was first reported in the late 1200s when Saint Francis of Assisi became the first known case. His hands, feet, and side bled; sometimes they bled more often than other times. The wounds were also very painful, as we know from Padre Pio's response when asked if they hurt. He said, "Do you think the Lord gave them to me as decoration?" The notoriety of these wounds, which Padre Pio did not like to show off or discuss, resulted in an almost cult following and stern rebuke from some church officials. Again, Padre Pio was to be a victim and he suffered in silence, as it was God's will.

The people in San Giovanni Rotondo grew to love their little saint. The archbishop, on the other hand, was not as enamored, nor were the secular priests. Although Pope Benedict XV found Padre Pio to be a humble and holy man, when he died and Pope Pius XI succeeded him, he was not as well informed on Padre Pio, as he would later admit. The persecution of Padre Pio within the church from certain members of the ecclesiastical hierarchy was intense. The backlash at San Giovanni Rotondo, and Padre Pio's pain at seeing what was happening due to things he never wanted for himself, were equally intense.

The Holy Office investigated the phenomena surrounding Padre Pio and declared that it could not confirm the authenticity of claims made of him. Beginning in 1922, various restrictions were placed on Padre Pio's ministry. Padre Pio was told to stop conversing by letter with his spiritual daughters. He was forbidden from hearing confessions, blessing crowds that gathered beneath his window, or showing anyone his wounds. He was not to allow the local women who flocked to him to kiss his hands. He was also forbidden from corresponding with his spiritual director, who was so important to the young priest. Ultimately, he was told he was not to celebrate Mass in public, but only by himself in the small chapel.

When word spread that Padre Pio might be transferred to another monastery, the town's people nearly rioted. A friend of Padre Pio threatened members of the Church leadership with exposing secrets of wrongdoing if they did not stop their persecution of Padre Pio. All of this pained Padre Pio who continued to suffer in silence. He told his friend, "You did a wicked thing! We must respect the decrees of the Church."

The persecution would continue until July 15, 1931, when Padre Pio was again permitted to celebrate Mass in public. The following year, he was again allowed to hear confessions of lay people.

His time in the confessional is as remarkable as all the other miraculous events attributed to him during his lifetime. He would often hear confessions for 18 hours a day. People would wait days to have Padre Pio hear their confessions. Many profess to have been converted and had their faith renewed due to their conversations with Padre Pio in the confessional and his administering of the sacrament. Of course, there were those who would go to Padre Pio out of pure curiosity. Padre Pio scolded the curiosity seekers and they left without absolution. Many later felt such remorse; they returned and made a good confession. Padre Pio worried about his temper in those moments, telling his provincial that he was concerned because he would "raise his voice" at such people.

For some, Padre Pio was able to read their souls. He would help them in making their confession, often telling them exactly what sins they had committed and how many times. He helped them open their hearts and souls to God and yearn for His forgiveness. His ministry in the confessional was an integral part of Padre Pio seeking to save souls and bring healing to people. It was as powerful as the stories of him appearing hundreds of miles away to visit someone or his healing of the sick.

Once restored to full ministry in 1934, Padre Pio began to focus on what he would call "The Work," the building of not just a hospital, but The House for the Relief of Suffering. He wanted a place where the sick could go and receive medical attention in an environment that respected the dignity of the person. His goal was to help people see the doctors and nurses as God's assistants in helping to alleviate their suffering.

In 1940, more formal discussions were had on his project. With World War II arriving the next year, it was not until 1947 that ground was broken on the road to where the Home would be situated. Funds were often tight, but they always came in so that in May 1956, the Home for the Relief of Suffering officially opened and was heralded by *The New York Times* as a facility like no other.

While Padre Pio's fame grew and he had a friend in Pope Pius XII, his difficulties were not over. In the 1960s, following Pius's death and Pope John XXIII's election, new rumors were spread about Padre Pio's ministry and his handling of the Home for the Relief of Suffering. Padre Pio was also deeply saddened by the lack of faith he saw in the people around him and in the clergy. Yet, Padre Pio's love of the Church never diminished and he held tightly to his conviction that we all owe obedience to the Church and her decrees, even when we may disagree with them.

On September 23, 1968, three days after the 50th anniversary of his receiving the stigmata, Padre Pio died. An examination of his body revealed no sign that the stigmata had ever been there. Other wounds, including scars from surgery, were present, but not the miraculous wounds he shared with the Lord.

Padre Pio followed God's path, becoming a priest, because of his faith, but also because of support from his parents and local priests. They set the first example for him. We need to do the same for our children.

Padre Pio also remained faithful to God's plan for him even when those closest to him seemed to abandon him, and he was faced with doubts about his own worthiness. In the face of outright hostility from his archbishop and decrees from the Vatican restricting his ministry, he did not abandon the Church, but respected her decrees as God's will. While few, especially in modern times, are as trusting and faithful, we are all called to such obedience. It resulted in the gift of Heaven for Padre Pio and the same promise is made to us.

Our path in life is not always easy. By faith, we know God is with us during the easy and hard times. To travel our journey, we need the gifts He gives us through the Church, its teachings and the sacraments. We all benefit from good, holy priests and, like the people of San Giovanni Rotondo and those who traveled around the world to see Padre Pio, we need to support our priests and pray that more will follow them in their ministry and walk with Christ. We all have a path to follow selected by God just for us. To find out what it is and to stay on it, we must Be Still … Be Not Afraid. To What is Jesus Calling You?

* * *

Many miracles are attributed to Padre Pio during his life. He is known to have had the gift of bilocation, where he appeared in a location hundreds of miles from San Giovanni Rotondo to give comfort to one in need, while at the same time others witnessed him in his room. He was known to bring about miraculous healings for incurable conditions. He read souls and told complete strangers the sins in their lives without them having to tell him anything. He was known to have visions of Jesus and the Blessed Mother and to be attacked by demons. His life is truly a miraculous one that even today's most faithful would have a hard time accepting. We have lost too much of the miraculous, the divine, but Padre Pio's life is proof that God still works in mysterious and extraordinary ways.

Still, the miracles attributed to Padre Pio during his lifetime cause some to forget his humble beginnings and the fact he was a man like any other. For the skeptic, they will use this aspect of his life as an excuse to dismiss Padre Pio all together and attribute these facts of his life to religious hysteria. Yet, Padre Pio was a faithful son of the Church, a priest who loved the Lord with his whole heart, mind, soul, his entire being.

God used Padre Pio to change people's lives, to remind them of God's love and to bring about the repentance of sins. Padre Pio suffered for the conversion of souls in a manner as close to Christ's ultimate suffering on the cross as a mortal person can suffer. The outward sign of the stigmata was a reminder for the world of Christ's sacrifice, while the pain Padre Pio suffered as a result of the stigmata connected him to Christ in a way that few have ever experienced.

It is in the confessional where we receive the sacrament for the forgiveness of our sins and it was there that Padre Pio made the most lasting impression on the souls he encountered. The words of absolution are those of Christ as the priest fulfills the duty the Lord gave to the apostles for the forgiveness of sins. Christ used a humble friar so people of great faith, or no faith at all, could encounter the Lord and receive His grace as their sins were wiped away. People would wait in line for days just to have Padre Pio hear their confession. In the end, they left in awe of God's great love knowing that the Lord had forgiven what they may have thought was unforgivable. It was this reconciliation with God that was the theme of Padre Pio's ministry and the theme of Padre Pio's life. It is what we are all called to, reconciliation with our Creator and our Savior by abandoning sin and embracing the Gospel.

When we walk with Christ, the miracles will happen even when all earthly powers are thrown at us to knock us off our path. But like Padre Pio, we must remain steadfast and humbly walk with God through any storm. Padre Pio suffered persecution from within the Church, not just from those who rejected Christ all together, but he accepted that suffering with such humility. How Padre Pio endured his trials, with great meekness and holy obedience, should be a lesson for all of us.

We do not just walk away from the Church because we were offended by the pastor, or our bishop, or the person who cut us off in the parking lot. We pray and endure and continue to follow Christ. In time, Padre Pio was restored to full ministry, even though skeptics remained. So, too, our trials will pass. If we are steadfast in following Jesus and remain faithful to His teaching as passed on through the authority He granted to the Church, we will experience His great love in the brightest of days and the darkest of nights of our lives.

Chapter 19

THERE IS NO question the Church needs holy priests. Their humility, sacrifice, and modeling of Christ's love are vital to spreading the faith and fostering holiness among the laity and the world. We have seen great examples of holiness in priests such as Padre Pio and Father Damien. For the parish priest, we need look no further than the patron of parish priests, Saint John Vianney.

SAINT JOHN VIANNEY
(May 2010)

As 2009 came to a close, the sky was the limit for Oakland Athletics' 23-year-old prospect Grant Desme. He had just come off two great seasons, finishing as the MVP and home run leader in the Arizona Fall League. There was talk that after another good season in the minors, he would get a call up to the major leagues in September. But God had other things in store for him. In January, Desme announced his retirement from baseball to enter the seminary to become a priest, which he will do in August. He told the team in 2007 when they made him a second round draft pick out of college that "above all, my faith comes first and I dedicate myself to church." Four months ago, the team and all of baseball learned what he meant. Desme's story reminds us what Saint John Vianney told us: "There are no two good ways of serving God. There is only one: serve Him as He desires to be served." Desme is on the path to do just that, following in the footsteps of Saint John Vianney, the only parish priest to be named a saint.

John Baptiste Marie Vianney was born and baptized May 8, 1786, the fourth of six children born to Christian parents in Dardilly, France. His father worked the fields of the family farm, land that had been in the family for a century. From the time he was old enough to walk, he joined his father and siblings in the fields, tending the sheep and cows. This good natured, blue-eyed, brown-haired boy learned about God's love at his mother's knee. Even though he received no formal schooling until the age of 17, this did not stop him from teaching catechesis to the other young shepherds, a skill that would serve him well later in life.

The Church and particularly her priests were the target of much persecution in France during the time of John's upbringing. Things were difficult in those years following the French revolution, but through disguise and transferring around, priests continued with their duty as best as possible. One such priest, working as a baker in the nearby village of Ecully, would prove to be instrumental in young John's desire to enter the priesthood.

This desire did not come as a flash from heaven, but was a gradual yearning of his heart, one that centered on John's desire to win souls for God. Still, to become a priest required a great deal of education, something John had none of. While his mother was supportive, it took John's father two years before he would support his request to enter the seminary. Father Balley, that priest from Ecully, took John in to get him started on his studies at the age of 20.

John struggled mightily in his studies, particularly in learning Latin, which made it difficult to understand what was being said in lectures or to answer questions from his professors. John even took a year off to decide if this difficult path was really for him.

In 1809, John was drafted into the army for the war in Spain. Napoleon was short on soldiers and even though seminarians were eligible for an exemption, John's name was not on the exempt list, so he had to report for duty. His parents tried to find a substitute with a promise of 3,000 francs and a gratuity, but the young man who was to take his place backed out at the last minute. As fate would have it, upon his arrival for military duty, John fell ill and was sent to the hospital. Upon his release, he found his troop had already headed for Spain. His efforts to catch up were in vain, with him again falling ill with a fever in the cold winter air. He was ultimately housed by the mayor of Les Noes, but he was now a deserter.

The following year, a decree was issued granting amnesty to deserters, a decree that covered John Vianney. He returned to Father Balley to continue his studies, but when his Latin failed to improve upon entry into the Grand Seminary, he was asked to leave after the first semester. Father Balley tutored him privately, refusing to let him fail. Still, John Vianney twice failed his examinations needed for ordination. After much perseverance, he was ultimately ordained on August 13, 1815.

In 1818, John Vianney was assigned to become the chaplain to a small country church in Ars, a short distance from Lyon in southern France. The village had about 40 homes and 230 souls. The Vicar-General told him upon giving him the assignment: "There is not much love in that parish—you will instill some into it." It is no wonder the young priest got lost trying to find the village.

When he arrived, John Vianney found a church in dire need of repair and a presbytery in need of even more. He set to work on the building and those who were to visit there. He told himself that one day the tiny church would not hold all the people who would flock there. He bought a new altar with his own money, painted the woodwork on the walls, and ultimately built new side chapels, one for the Blessed Mother, to whom he was greatly devoted, and where he celebrated Mass every Saturday for 41 years. He also replaced the furniture, vestments, and vessels, all in sad need of repair. The priest in the tattered cassock bought the best for the church as a sign to those who would come to receive what awaited for them inside.

During his time, religious fervor and knowledge of Church teaching were lacking. Most people worked on Sundays rather than dedicate themselves to celebrating the Lord's day. Taverns were numerous in Ars, places the new priest declared were "the devil's own shop, the market where souls are bartered, and where the harmony of families is broken up, where quarrels start and murders are done." He challenged the local people's culture, their way of life and called them back to love of God. He visited the sick, helped the poor, and walked the fields to meet the people. Whether they wanted him to or not, John Vianney made it his business to meet all people and teach them wherever he found them.

At first, many did not take too kindly to his stern warnings over their wayward behavior, making many false claims against him. In spite of all the suffering he endured, over time, the village of Ars changed. Rather than work the fields on Sunday evening, people began overflowing the church for Vespers. The taverns even had to close for lack of patrons. When it was learned that the Vicar-General was going to move their young priest, the people paid him a visit and quickly convinced him to keep John Vianney there and name him pastor.

John Vianney understood clearly that if he was going to win over the people and convert sinners, he had to model what he taught. His life had to be a witness to Christ in all things, and that is just what he did. With frequent fasts, simple living, self-mortification for the repentance of sins, and always being available, people flocked to hear his preaching. As the people said, "Our priest always does what he says himself; he practices what he preaches." John Vianney even opened a school for girls called "Providence" where he would teach the catechism daily and take his dinner, which for him was often just a few boiled potatoes and black bread. He slept less than four hours a day.

His favorite books were his breviary and the Lives of the Saints. He often told people of the lives of saints to inspire them to live a life of Christ. He spent hours working on his sermons, applying the basic tenets of faith to the world in which he lived. When asked his secret by fellow priests who were not having much success in transforming their parishes, John Vianney answered "You have preached, you have prayed, but have you fasted? Have you taken the discipline (a self imposed scourge)? Have you slept on the floor? So long as you have done none of these things, you have no right to complain." If the priest was not completely dedicated to Christ and His work in converting souls, doing whatever it took and facing any opposition, then the devil would prevail and that was unacceptable.

John Vianney preached the importance of receiving Christ in the Eucharist, that most precious of sacraments. He was often seen praying before the tabernacle. To receive the Eucharist, John Vianney knew the souls of the people needed to be freed from sin and that was accomplished only through the Sacrament of Reconciliation. The confessional was a solid box placed in the middle of the church with no windows. In the summer, it was stifling hot and in the winter, bone chilling cold, but John spent up to 12 hours a day in the winter and 16 hours a day in the summer hearing confessions. The renewal of this sacrament is what ultimately converted people's souls and transformed their lives and those of the community.

John Vianney was known to read souls and see the needs of people even before they spoke. At times, when someone started walking away because of the long lines, he came out and called them back, recognizing their needs even though they had never met. He recounted undisclosed sins and saw the greatest needs of their souls. To the sincere, he was a great comfort; to the curious, he challenged them to take a serious look at their lives. For some, seeing the tears streaming down the priest's face during confession left the most profound impact. When asked why he cried upon hearing their sins, he said, "My friend, I weep because you do not weep."

John Vianney preached about the dangers of sin and the importance of dedicating all aspects of our lives to Jesus. He challenged people to live differently—to live as if their lives depended on how they lived their faith, because it does.

During the last years of his life, the city of Lyon had to find a way to accommodate the nearly 100,000 people who flocked to Ars each year just to hear John Vianney preach or have him hear their confessions. This included bishops and dignitaries. The train station issued passes to Ars good for eight days because it often took several days for people to get through the lines to have Father Vianney hear their confessions. After all, he was hearing between 300 to 400 confessions a day in a town of less than 250.

With all the graces coming to the people through Father Vianney's work, the devil was there, too. John Vianney was terrorized at night with loud and haunting noises. On one occasion, when he was coming out of the confessional, a parishioner told him that his room was on fire. The priest responded that the devil, unable to catch the bird, had decided to burn the cage. Things were worse just before a great conversion, yet God always won.

Eventually, the demonic sounds stopped and the flocks of pilgrims increased until John Vianney died at two a.m. on August 4, 1859. His greatest miracle was his life, a life that helped bring thousands out of sin and back to a life of God.

Saint John Vianney, the Cure of Ars, was canonized on May 31, 1925, and is the patron saint of parish priests. Saint John Vianney recognized how important the priest was and how difficult his life could be, so he constantly promoted a life of prayer, fasting, and penance as the way to remain fully in love with Christ and faithful to his calling. When Pope Benedict XVI announced 2010 as the Year of the Priest in honor of the 150th anniversary of Saint John Vianney's death, he exhorted all priests to follow the saint's example. He recognized the indispensable role of the priest. First, the Pope cautioned, "How can we forget, in this regard, that nothing causes more suffering for the Church, the Body of Christ, than the sins of her pastors, especially the sins of those who become 'thieves and robbers' of the sheep, lead them astray by their own private teachings, or ensnare them in the toils of sin and death?" Priests need our prayers and encouragement to be that perfect model of faith. Without the priest, we do not have the sacraments and the graces that flow from them. As the Pope concluded, "The Church needs holy priests, ministers capable of helping the faithful to experience the Lord's merciful love, and convinced witnesses of that love."

We are all called to model the faith we received at our Baptism and to answer God's call in our lives. The example of Saint John Vianney is as important for us as it is for our priests. We must pray, fast, and do penance to remain close to God. We must be completely dedicated to God in all things and serve Him as He calls us to serve. For some, that is answering the call to the priesthood and religious life. Whether we are on the verge of stardom, or tending the family farm, through prayer and the sacraments and maybe even the example of our parish priest, we will learn of God's plan for our lives and have the courage to answer the call. So Be Still, Be Not Afraid ... To What is Jesus Calling You?

* * *

Saint John Vianney faced many obstacles in his life and ministry. Some were small and annoying and others quite imposing. In the end, they were all put there to keep him from accomplishing Christ's mission of love and conversion. By remaining steadfast and seeing the obstacles for the petty annoyances they were, Saint John Vianney discovered how easy they were to overcome by remaining faithful to Jesus' call and his vocation as a priest. Saint John Vianney knew that Satan does not want holy priests, holy mothers and holy fathers, holy single people, or holy children, so he puts obstacles in our path to divert our attention from what is really important. Most of these obstacles have no substance to them whatsoever, which we quickly discover by remaining on our path toward heaven.

Saint John Vianney persevered in the face of such obstacles. He was greeted with a church in need of repair, both physically and spiritually. He was faced with a laity that took their faith casually, but he challenged them with the fullness of the faith, not a watered down version hoping to win friends. Saint John Vianney was about winning souls for Christ, and to do so, he had to teach the whole of God's Truth, even it was difficult for the people to hear. After all, one of the things he called them to do was to leave their pubs and pints on Sunday and return to Church, to prayer, confession, and a life of virtue.

Saint John Vianney was also faced with demons who sought to scare him from his ministry. Nothing deterred Saint John Vianney, however, and souls were brought home to God. What a wonderful and glorious testimony Saint John Vianney gave to the Truth of Jesus Christ. People were brought back to the faith, to confessing their sins and being reconciled to God, and receiving the Eucharist more worthily. The people of Ars and those who traveled there to hear Saint John Vianney preach or have him hear their confession came to rediscover Jesus, the Messiah and Savior of the world. We should all strive to leave such a legacy.

We learn from Saint John Vianney that the institution of the priesthood is constantly under attack. This is the institution that brings us the sacraments, the gifts from Christ that feed our souls and give true hope, true peace, true strength. Yet, the notion of the priesthood remains under attack as it has been since Jesus established the priest with the first Apostles. It is under attack from the sins of some who took the vows of priesthood and from an increasingly secular society that fails to understand the importance and beauty of the priesthood and religious life. Yet, the greatest gift the Church gives to a community and a parish is a holy priest who makes Jesus present, not just in the sacrament of the altar, the Eucharist, but in how he lives and how he interacts with people.

We need to pray for our priests and encourage more young men to follow this vocation. Many who are called fail to answer for any number of reasons, often failing to see the minor obstacles for what they are and therefore turn back. But, the seed of faith sowed by Jesus is good seed and will produce good fruit. We need to nurture those seeds of faith in ourselves, our family and friends, and everyone we meet. We must prepare the soil of souls of our young people and ourselves regardless of age to experience God in all things and follow Him on the path He selects for us. We cannot walk a more beautiful, rewarding, exciting, or challenging path than the one God lays before us. After all, the path God chooses for us leads to heaven, the greatest and only destination worth seeking.

Saint John Vianney taught that we are to serve God as He calls us to serve Him. That is our path. There is no promise that following that path will protect us from all suffering or trouble, for we are called to pick up our cross and carry it as we travel this path. Suffering comes to those who love, and we are called to love. This is true whether we are a priest, policeman, or politician, whether married or single, no matter our vocation in life. Saint John Vianney teaches us to trust in the Lord and that our life must belong to Christ and to Him alone. When we do, all else takes care of itself.

Chapter 20

HOLY WOMEN ARE just as vital to the Church's mission as holy priests. The Church was founded on both and needs both to carry out the mission entrusted to her by Christ. We know that from the Church's founding, women have played an important role in spreading the faith. While the head of the Church was entrusted to men, it may be said that the heart of the Church was entrusted to women.

Women religious foster the mission of the Church in many ways. Some are like Saint Therese of Lisieux and spend their lives within the convent praying for the conversion of sinners and for priests. Living a life quietly and obscurely, but in total dedication to Christ, brings holiness to the world. Some are like Saint Elizabeth Ann Seton and dedicate their lives to the teaching of children. Passing on the fullness of God's Truth through the teachings of the Church is at the heart of the Church's mission of evangelization. Some are like Mother Teresa who care for the sick, the outcast, the forgotten, the dying. They share God's love with those the Lord holds most dear.

Women religious have started hospitals, schools, and social service agencies that help those in need with the love and compassion of Jesus Christ. These women have helped countless millions of all faiths, and no faith, experience God's healing touch. They support the local church and the ministry of the universal Church. Yet, not all women religious function in the social justice ministries of the Church and women are not relegated to those ministries.

Throughout the Church's history, voices of renewal are heard. These voices belong to women and to men who carry on and remind the Church of Christ's call to conversion. As with the prophets, these saints call all of us to repentance and conversion. Indeed, during a very dark time in the world and for the Church, kings and popes listened to and headed the call of one courageous woman religious to once again return to faithfully living the Gospel of Jesus Christ—to remember that all the baptized are called to follow Christ in all things, and that they are all part of the One Body of Christ. When the Lord needed to get everyone's attention, he called on Saint Catherine of Siena.

SAINT CATHERINE OF SIENA
(August 2010)

In Saint Mark's Gospel, we read that Jesus "summoned the crowd with his disciples and said to them, 'Whoever wishes to come after me must deny himself, take up his cross, and follow me. For whoever wishes to save his life will lose it, but whoever loses his life for my sake and that of the gospel will save it.'" (Mk 8:34-35). During a time in the Church's history that can only be described as filled with turmoil, one young girl chose from the earliest of ages to lose herself for Christ so that she might live for Him and bring about reform for the Church and the world in which she lived.

Catherine was born on March 25, 1347, in Siena, Italy. She was the 24th of 25 children born to Giacomo and Lapa Benincasa. Her twin sister died at birth and the youngest was born a year later during the plague and did not survive. Her father was a dyer and although they lived in a poor part of town, the entire family lived in a sprawling home to accommodate such a large family. Catherine was a joyful child who learned all she could about God. One family tradition was hearing about the lives of the saints.

At the age of six, Catherine had her first experience with the divine. When she and her brother were returning home from a visit with an older, married sister, Catherine saw a vision of Jesus sitting on a throne flanked by the Apostles Peter, Paul and John. The vision appeared just above the Church of Saint Dominic. Her heart was overflowing with love for her

Savior who looked upon her and blessed her. When her brother, who had continued on, returned to find her gazing at the sky and called out to her, she turned away from the vision to answer him. When she returned her gaze to the spot where she had seen Jesus, the vision was gone. She was sad and felt guilty for having turned her thoughts away from the Lord.

From that day forward, Catherine belonged to Jesus. At the age of seven, she made a solemn vow to God to remain perpetually a virgin, dedicating her life only to Him. She would fast and pray often. She was always joyful, even when scolded. In deciding which order to join for her vocation, Catherine focused on the Order of Preachers, the Dominicans. In the tradition of Saint Dominic, they were known to go out and preach the gospel everywhere for the conversion of souls and the protection of the Church. Little could she know at this young age how God would use her in precisely that fashion.

Around the age of 12, her parents were looking forward to Catherine preparing herself for marriage, as was the custom of the time. Catherine, however, had no inclination to marry, for she belonged entirely to Jesus. When her parents' persuasion failed, they tried punishment, making her share a room so she would not be alone and having her serve in the kitchen for the entire family. Rather than obtain the desired effect, Catherine relished her service to the family. When her brother was asleep, she would kneel upon her bed in prayer for most of the night.

Exasperated at her unwillingness to make herself available to possible suitors, Catherine's mother called on Father Tommaso della Fonte, a Dominican friar, to talk to Catherine. When he did so, the friar understood Catherine's calling at once and told her, "The moment you are absolutely sure you want to serve the Lord exclusively and your parents urge you to do otherwise, show them how steadfast is your determination by cutting off your hair. Then, perhaps, they will quiet down." At the age of 15, Catherine did just that and cut off her hair to the horrified cries of her mother.

After dinner one night, she confronted her family with her decision. She had made her choice after mature reflection and prayer that she should belong completely to Jesus. She told her family that they should stop insisting that she marry because she was going to obey God and not men. Silence fell over the household and then her father, with tears in his eyes, said that her desire would be done, telling her "God forbid, my dear daughter, that we should in any way contradict the divine Will, from which, as we all realize, comes your holy intention. At last we are certain that you are not moved by the caprice of youth, but by an impulse of divine love. Fulfill your vow, then, by holy plans and we shall not interfere. Pray for us, so that we may be worthy of the promise of your Betrothed Whom, by His grace, you chose in your earliest years."

The Sisters of Penance of the Third Order of Saint Dominic consisted primarily of older women in Siena who lived in their own homes. They agreed to speak with Catherine and after she answered all of their questions satisfactorily, they accepted her. At the age of 16 in the Church of Saint Dominic, she was invested with the holy habit. Her novitiate would be like no other in that Jesus and Mary would be her teachers. Catherine would continue to live at home and wear the habit, but for the next three years, she would eat and sleep little and speak to no one. Her days were filled with prayer, penance, fasting, and frequent visions of Jesus teaching her of His great love and the love she must have for others. In return, Catherine exclaimed, "My God, my All."

At the age of 20, she had another vision of Christ in which her spiritual betrothal was manifested by a ring being placed upon her finger for only her to see, to remind her that she belonged to Jesus. He then told her that, to truly love, she must love others as He has loved her, with tenderness, mercy, and for no other reason than that God loved that person, as well. Thus, her life was to be one of service to others.

Catherine spent the next several years helping the poor and the ill. She amassed a great number of followers who were drawn to her by her purity. Catherine became what she would call herself: "A servant and slave of the servants of Jesus Christ." She was known to give to the poor whatever they needed, even taking the clothes off her own back. She would visit the sick in their distress, even during the great plague. During this time, one of her earliest followers was the head of the hospital. He fell ill with the plague while in church and was taken to the hospital. On death's door, Catherine went to see him and upon entering his room said, "Get up, sir, this is no time to be lying comfortably in bed." At once he was healed.

Catherine would even visit sick sisters and patients who would berate her, but she served them with such joy and such faithfulness that they were converted. She even converted condemned prisoners. More and more, people of high and low estate, from kings and popes to the poor and downcast, sought out this young virgin of Siena. With all the good work she was doing, gossip and stories were bound to spread. None were true, but Catherine, in spite of such scandalous allegations, treated everyone with charity. When someone came to challenge her teaching, he left convinced she was without error. She had the ability to know what others were doing and when, so as to tell them their sins. Her humility and faithfulness drew people to her.

Catherine's visions of Christ continued throughout her life as He was her teacher. She sought to receive communion daily and was often found in ecstasy. She was so horrified of sin and the loss of a soul that she took it personally and asked that the Lord punish her for another falling into sin.

In 1375, Catherine was praying for a priest who was going through a crisis of faith. One day while praying after communion, Catherine asked the Lord if He would promise to grant her prayer. The Lord asked her to extend her hand. When she did, it was pierced with a nail. Later that year, in Pisa, while again praying after communion, rays appeared from the crucifix, coming from the nails in the Lord's hands and feet and the wound in his side. Catherine, too, was pierced by the rays. While the stigmata was not visible on Catherine's body until after she died, the pain associated with sharing in Christ's suffering was very real for her, a suffering she longed to endure for the salvation of souls.

Many priests became spiritual sons of Catherine. They traveled with her wherever she went because people, after their conversion, sought to go to confession so they could then receive the Eucharist. The priests were often hearing confessions continuously for days on end. Her influence among people to return to a life of service to God and the Church was extensive. She desired holy priests, holy sisters, and holy people who yearned for God and would share His love with their neighbors. Because of her influence, she was highly sought after for consultation in political matters of the time, including matters involving the Pope.

To understand the world in which Saint Catherine lived, it is helpful to understand the political and spiritual climate of the time. In the 14th Century, the Church was suffering from external pressures and internal corruption. The Pope had been residing in Avignon, France since 1309, and was seen as being under the influence of the French king. There was constant tension between secular leaders and the Papacy. War was widespread among Christians. In 1373, Pope Gregory XI declared another Crusade to help free the Holy Land from the Turks, but there was never enough unity among the faithful for such an endeavor because all over Europe Christians were fighting Christians, and many were aligned against the Pope. Cardinals and bishops were acting more like war lords than shepherds. Priests were not teaching what the Church taught and lived in luxury and vice. Still, the people craved God's love and grace and respected the sacraments immensely. Calming tensions between states and cities and the Pope, returning the Pope to Rome and the See of Saint Peter, and reforming the Church hierarchy to one of spiritual purity were all goals Catherine would strive to achieve. She knew that there were few hours left in her life to accomplish this important work, so she was quick about it.

Pope Gregory XI, having heard of Catherine's great holiness, sought out her advice. Catherine wrote to the Pope to encourage him to reform the Church. Pope Gregory wanted just that, but he was not strong enough to bring it about. Catherine's message to the Pope was that he was the Vicar of Christ and must exhibit and demand holiness, especially from his legates, cardinals, bishops, and clergy. Catherine encouraged the Pope to clean house, all the way down to the foundation, if necessary, to bring back holiness to the Church. The Church's treasure was not silver and gold, but the Blood of Christ. There needed to be holiness of conscience and in institutions. Catherine knew that regardless of the scandals that would come with such reform that Christ would rid the Church of the evil that infected it and the true light of Christ would shine forth.

Pope Gregory failed to heed this early advice as was evidenced by his next selection of cardinals. There were revolts and resulting excommunications. These struggles and the resulting crisis of credibility in the Pope was a direct result of a lack of holiness. To put down revolts, cardinals were employing bandits for hire who committed atrocities as great as those they went to subdue. Through all this, one of the biggest fights was with Florence. Ultimately, both sides asked for Catherine's help in bringing about peace.

Catherine met first with the Florentines. Her goal always began with the conversion of the soul and a rejection of sin. She told them that the Pope was Christ's Vicar on earth and must be followed. The merit of the man who served as Pope was not the issue, but the fact he was the Successor of Saint Peter was what mattered. She told the people they cannot revolt against the Church, for the Church "is Christ Himself and she dispenses the sacraments and gives us life." While it was acceptable to call out a member who was corrupt, the Church herself is not corrupt any more than Christ is corrupt. Further, governments remained under God's law and were to serve the common good rather than their own self interests.

Catherine then met with Pope Gregory XI. She encouraged him to show compassion and mercy to bring the people of Florence back into the Church's family. She implored the Pope to make peace with Florence and also to return to Rome where he belonged. A resurgence of holiness was needed to save Europe, which was in danger of collapse, both from the Turks and internal fighting. This was the primary reason Catherine encouraged the Pope to proceed with the Crusade and for civic leaders and hired marauders to unite behind the Pope. But the Pope's political missteps doomed any prospect of a Crusade and continued to be an obstacle to peace.

Catherine finally won over the Pope to show mercy to Florence and make peace. Florence, on the other hand, only caused more revolt. As a result, things got worse. In 1376, the Pope essentially shut down Florence. All churches closed and there were no services. The loss of commercial and political interests that came with recognition by the Church was deeply felt in Florence.

Even with the apparent lack of progress towards peace, during all of her diplomacy, Catherine did win one major victory; the Pope finally returned to Rome on January 17, 1377, much to the dismay of the French cardinals. Given the political climate, the Pope feared he would receive a hostile reception, but his reception proved to be just the opposite and resembled Christ's triumphal entry into Jerusalem. The fight with Florence, however, continued.

Catherine returned to Florence in 1378 during another uprising. This time, a group of locals turned on Catherine and accused her of working for the Pope against Florence. When they came and found her in a garden with some of her followers, they asked for her with the intent of killing her. She approached and said she was Catherine and that they may kill her, but they must promise to not harm any of the others with her. The man leading the group hesitated and then ran off, followed by the rest. Catherine wept, for she saw the event as evidence that she was not faithful enough for martyrdom.

Later that year, Catherine dictated her "Dialogue of Divine Providence." In it, she has a conversation with God and presents four requests for mercy, one for herself, one for the world, one for the Church, and one for a particular case. It is an overwhelming dialogue on Love. Her "Dialogue" and the over 400 letters she wrote that are left to us today explain why she was declared a Doctor of the Church.

The days for the Church were only getting darker. In 1379, Pope Gregory XI died at the age of 49. There was a call from the people for a Roman Pontiff and the cardinals felt threatened as they entered the conclave. Out of it came Pope Urban VI, an Italian, although not Roman. He was strong in pushing for reform, especially within the clergy, but his manner upset many, including those who had become accustomed to living in luxury.

It did not take long before 13 of the 16 cardinals left Rome for Avignon and declared they were forced to elect Pope Urban, making his election invalid. As a sign of defiance and what was the beginning of a great schism, they elected an anti-pope, Clement VII. Christendom was split as different sections aligned behind either Pope Urban VI or the anti-pope, Clement VII. The schism would last until 1417 and the Council of Constance.

Catherine continued to work for peace and conversion. She preached and demonstrated holiness. She demanded fidelity to Christ and His Church. While she would not see the peace she longed for in her lifetime, Catherine's mark on the Church was indelible as the number of the faithful of all statures influenced by her holiness testifies.

On January 29, 1380, Catherine collapsed while praying in church. She was not eating at all. On February 26, the Third Week of Lent, her followers gathered around her to hear what she had to say to them. She prayed for their lives to be dedicated to Christ and the reform of His Church.

Catherine remained in bed until Easter Sunday, March 25, which was also her 33rd birthday, when she suddenly got up and went to Mass. Her strength left her after the service. On April 29, 1380, she called her closest followers together for the last time. When she had finished talking to them, she looked skyward and said, "Father, into thine hands I commend my spirit." With that, she died.

Catherine's entire life was dedicated to serving Christ completely. She had no regard for her own well-being, but only for serving Christ by serving others and His Church. Her message to others was simple and direct; we must live for Christ and for Christ alone. Unless we die to self, we cannot live for Him who gives us life. All of the turmoil for the Church in her day, which overwhelms the crises and scandals we are dealing with today, could be solved by people returning to Christ and living holy lives. It was this call to holiness, which applied to the Pope, cardinals, clergy, religious, kings, and laity alike, and a soul's connection with its Savior, which were most important to her. She sought reforms out of love, she sought peace out of love, she sought conversion of souls out of love, for God is love.

We too are called to be faithful and to live lives of holiness. To truly love, we must forget ourselves and live for Christ. We love completely when we love others because of our love of Christ. God asked much of Catherine in her short life, and when she said "Yes" to Him, He gave her everything she needed to accomplish the daunting tasks He set out for her. While she did not get to see the full fruits of her labor, she witnessed common, everyday people returning to God and His Church and the Pope returning to the See of Rome, where the first Vicar, Saint Peter, laid down his life for Christ. Catherine discovered God's plan for her in the quiet of her prayers and in trusting in God's great love. We are called to do the same to learn of God's call in our lives. So remember to Be Still … Be Not Afraid, To What is Jesus Calling You?

* * *

Saint Catherine developed a following by boldly speaking the truth. She did not water it down for all of Christ's commands are made out of love for His people. If we remain faithful to the Lord's teaching, we remain close to Him.

There is Truth. Christ calls us to follow Him, not our image of Him, not our desire of what we wish He had said, not what we think He might say if He lived today. There is right and there is wrong; there is goodness and holiness and there is sin and evil. Personal desires often obscure the difference and create many shades of gray. When we die to self and live for Christ, picking up our cross everyday to follow Him, then making the right choices is easier. All of our actions have consequences. As Christians, we are called to follow Christ regardless of the circumstances, regardless of our social status, regardless of the consequences. If we are to save our lives, we must be willing to lose them for Christ.

All people, from the Pope to your neighbor across the street, are called by their Baptism to follow Jesus. Saint Catherine understood what God's kingdom was to look like and how we could make that vision a reality. To bring about the peace, joy, and love Christ preached, we had but one path to follow and that was to follow The Way, the Truth, and The Life. Power and worldly concerns can cause us to turn our gaze and our thoughts away from Jesus, so that when we return our gaze to the spot where we last recall seeing Jesus, we may not find Him. Still, as Saint Catherine understood well, Jesus continues to wait for us, continues to call to us to return to Him and follow Him.

For the kingdom of God to shine in our times, we must set the example and live our faith, our faith in Christ Jesus as He is and as He taught us. That requires sacrifice because we cannot be driven by our own self desires, but only by living for Christ. There are no new apps to buy, no new gadgets to acquire, just a conversion of heart and a determination to remain faithful to Christ who has taught us all we need to know.

Chapter 21

SAINT CATHERINE'S GREATEST influence on the Church, from popes to common, everyday people, was her life of holiness. There was another who preceded her whose holiness is known the world over. From Saint Catherine of Siena to Saint Francis of Assisi, we learn that the best way to teach the Gospel is to first live holy lives, for then the Gospel will come alive, not only in ourselves, but in those we meet.

SAINT FRANCIS OF ASSISI
(October 2010)

"A young man came to Jesus to ask Him what he must do to receive eternal life. When Jesus told him to obey the commandments, the young man said, 'All of these I have observed. What do I still lack?' Jesus said to him, 'If you wish to be perfect, go sell what you have and give to the poor, and you will have treasure in heaven. Then come, follow me.' When the young man heard this statement, he went away sad, for he had many possessions." (Matt 19:16-30). For another young man, however, the Lord's statement was a joy and he began his life in Christ by giving away all he had, and lived the remainder of his life as the Little Poor Man from Assisi.

Francis was born in 1181, the older of two sons born to Pietro and Pica Bernadone. Francis was of medium height, slight build, large dark eyes, and had a merry disposition. His father was a well to do textile merchant in

France. From this influence, Francis was enamored with the French troubadours and their songs of bravery and love of their maidens. His dream was to become a famous knight, known for his bravery in battle.

With war common, it would not be long before Francis would experience combat first hand. In 1198, the merchant class of Assisi revolted against the nobility, causing them to flee to nearby Perugia. In 1202, Perugia launched an assault to win Assisi back. The two warring cities met on a hilltop that lay between them. The battle was brutal and bloody, with Assisi being routed. Francis was taken captive, presumably because he was viewed as a prisoner who could fetch a ransom.

Francis was held prisoner for a year. The conditions were terrible and Francis's health suffered greatly, but his upbeat spirit never left him, much to the surprise of his captors and fellow prisoners. Upon his release, he returned home. His recovery was slow, but eventually he resumed working with his father and socializing with his friends.

Francis was quite popular. With a well to do father, Francis was often chosen as the King of Fools who not only paid for all the food and drink at the party, but also carried the scepter as the band of young people wandered the streets singing and merrymaking.

In 1204, a French knight, Gautier de Biene came looking for men to join him in battle against the Normans. Francis jumped at the chance to go to war and headed off with other starry eyed young men to meet up with the famous knight. Francis made it 15 miles to Spoleto where his journey ended. He came down with a fever and missed the others moving out the next morning. A dream told him to return to Assisi. While people were surprised to see him back so soon, Francis kept up his spirits. His return was providential, for Gautier and his men were slaughtered in battle.

Francis had returned a changed man. He spent more time in prayer and meditation and less time working in his father's shop or partying with his friends. He was drawn to helping the poor and often gave them food and clothing.

The year 1206 was an important one in the conversion of Francis. He took a pilgrimage to Rome to visit the tomb of Saint Peter. While there, he noticed all the beggars in front of the basilica that housed his tomb. Francis traded his clothes with one of the beggars and often sat and ate with them.

Later that year, Francis was on a trip for his father when he came upon a leper crossing the road and shaking a stick to warn anyone in the area of his presence. Francis, repulsed by the sight and smell of lepers, turned around. Guilt then overwhelmed him. As the man was walking way, Francis ran after him and embraced him. His inhibitions were gone and he could see the image of Christ in the poor, in their suffering, and in his own suffering.

These experiences prepared him for his next encounter with Christ still later in the year. While passing the small church of San Damiano just south of Assisi, Francis stopped to pray. While in prayer, the Crucifix spoke to Francis and said, "Francis, go repair my house, which, as you can see, is falling completely into ruin." The fullness of the message was lost on Francis, but he rushed to gather the funds needed to repair the small church.

Francis went to his father's shop, took rolls of fabrics and the horse, and set off to a market ten miles away. He sold all of his goods, including the horse, and walked back to Assisi. Upon returning to San Damiano, Francis presented the money to the priest who refused to take it. Francis left the money on the window sill.

Francis's father was furious with his son and demanded that his money be returned. Francis hid from his father out of fear. After a while, he knew he had to return to Assisi. Upon seeing him, many in the city started making fun of him, causing a scene in the public square. When Pietro Bernadone heard the noise, he went to see what was happening. Upon seeing his son, Pietro really lost his temper and grabbed Francis, dragging him home where he was imprisoned in a room. His mother released him while his father was away on a trip. His father was not happy when he discovered his son gone upon his return.

The missing property was not resolved until the following spring when Pietro was forced to call upon the bishop for assistance. The hearing on the matter took place in the plaza before the bishop's residence. Pietro made his case, demanding the return of everything that belonged to him. The bishop then looked at Francis and told him that if he was to follow God, he needed to return the property, which he had no right to take. Francis then walked into the bishop's house and returned almost naked, holding his clothes and the money bag. Upon dropping them at his father's feet, Francis said, "Listen to me, everybody! Up until now, I have called Pietro Bernadone my father. But now that I propose to serve God, I give him back, not only this money that he wants so much, but all the clothes I have from him. From now on, I can advance naked before the Lord, saying in truth no longer my father Pietro Bernadone, but Our Father who art in heaven." His father collected the items and left.

Francis returned to San Damiano where he learned to beg for food and beg for stones to repair the church. He preached in the city square and occasionally in church. He wore only the old tunic the gardener at the bishop's house gave him, adorning it with a cross he drew on the front. Francis also restored a place known as Portiuncula and its chapel, Mary Queen of Angels. This latter location would hold special significance to Francis and his new order.

The ridicule of the Little Poor Man died off as people heard him preach, so moved were they by his words and his example. Francis came to realize his calling was to rebuild the spirit of the Church with souls and not just her buildings with stones. Before long, others began to follow his harsh and austere life. The first was Bernard of Quintavalle, a wealthy citizen of Assisi. He asked Francis what he needed to do to follow in his footsteps. After consulting the Gospels, Bernard, with Francis's help, gave all he had to the poor. Bernard remained with Francis throughout the saint's life.

Before long, dozens of men had left all they had to live the Gospel way of life and embrace holy poverty. To lend credibility to his band of brothers, Francis was encouraged to seek approval from the Pope for his Rule for the order. He went to see Pope Innocent III, who desperately wanted reform in the Church, but had seen too many insincere reformers. Ultimately, Francis's humility and God's intervention won the day, and the Order of Friars Minor was born.

The Friars Minor were to own nothing, greet everyone with "The Lord give you peace," preach repentance of sins, work with their hands, and resist no one. They were to follow the disciples' example and take nothing with them and accept only what was offered in exchange for their labor. They served lepers and accepted the hospitality of monks. On one occasion, a leper was very near death and of such a foul disposition that he cursed and drove all the friars away. Then Francis went to see him. After a few minutes, the man told Francis that he wanted Francis to bathe him since his rotting flesh smelled so badly. As Francis began to wash the man's body with clean, warm water, his sores disappeared and his suffering went away. The man's condition eventually returned, but he died in peace and later appeared to Francis to assure him of the man's salvation.

One of Francis's early followers was to begin an order of female friars minor. Any discussion of Francis is incomplete without a mention of Clare, who was so dear to him and upon whom he counted for advice and spiritual companionship. At the age of 15, Clare, who was ten years Francis's junior, left home and came to Portiuncula to embrace a life of poverty, prayer, and service. Francis accepted her into the order. She would make her home at San Damiano and found the Poor Clares.

The growth of the Friars Minor was remarkable. Their influence was seen in the laity and in the clergy alike. Their humble preaching and Christian charity changed souls. With their rapid growth, difficulties arose, including how to minister to the several thousand who joined the order during the saint's lifetime and complaints that the Rule was too harsh. These challenges weighed heavily on Francis.

The Friars Minor traveled to Christian and pagan lands to preach. Sometimes they were welcomed, while other times they were beaten and even killed. Francis wanted to participate in the Crusades to rescue the Holy Land from the Saracens. This he would do in 1219.

While with the knights, Francis foretold a horrible defeat and warned the troops to not go into battle. They mocked him, but the defeat was just as Francis predicted. Still, he brought hope and joy to those on the Crusade because he would tell them of both victories and defeats. For Francis, the thought of converting the Muslims to Christ was an opportunity he could not pass up.

Francis and another brother then set out to meet the Sultan. Upon being captured, they were beaten, chained, and taken to the Sultan. The Sultan covered the floor with crosses as a test. If Francis walked on them, he would accuse the saint of trampling on the cross, and if he refused, he would accuse him of insulting the Sultan for not wanting to approach him.

Francis walked over the crosses and when questioned, Francis said there were three crosses on Calvary, the one belonging to Christ, which he adores, and the others belonging to the thieves, which are perfectly fine for walking on if the Sultan would so choose. The Sultan was taken in by Francis, but refused to convert to Christianity. When Francis suggested a test to reveal the Truth by putting Francis and the Sultan's priests in a furnace as in the Old Testament, the priests fled and the Sultan would not allow Francis to prove the power of God in such a fashion. In the end, Francis left disappointed, but the Sultan asked him to pray for him.

In 1224, Francis and a few brothers set out for La Verna, about a hundred miles to the north of Assisi. It is a tall mountain with a monastery at the top open to the Friars. Upon arrival, Francis asked for a hut to be built outside, which was more to his custom than the fortification of the monastery. He prayed fervently and was often found in ecstasy.

On the Feast of the Assumption, Francis began a 40-day fast. He moved his hut to a small overhang reachable only by putting a tree over a large ravine. He told the friars that only Brother Leo could visit and then only twice a day, once to bring bread and water and the second for prayers at midnight. In his prayers, Francis pleaded, "O Lord, I beg of You two graces before I die—to experience in myself in all possible fullness the pains of Your cruel Passion, and to feel for You the same love that made You sacrifice Yourself for us." On the Feast of the Exaltation of the Cross, September 14, 1224, Francis's prayer was answered. He had a vision of Christ crucified in the form of a seraphim. The vision imprinted on Francis the wounds of Christ, the nail marks in his hands and feet and the wound in his side. The wounds of the stigmata would remain for the rest of his life.

Francis died on October 3, 1226, but not before dictating his Last Testament. In it, which reads as a letter to all Christians of all generations, Francis implores his brothers to stay true to the Rule he originally established that was accepted by the Pope. He prays for all to be drawn closer to Christ. As for the honor of the priesthood, Francis wrote: "Listen, my brothers. If the Blessed Virgin Mary is justly honored for having carried the Lord in her most chaste womb, if Saint John trembled at baptizing Him, not daring as it were, to place his hand on God's Chosen One; if the tomb wherein Jesus reposed for a few hours is the object of such veneration; then how worthy, virtuous, and holy ought he to be who touches with his fingers, receives in his mouth and in his heart, and administers to others, Christ, no longer mortal, but eternally triumphant and glorious! Let every man tremble, let the whole world shake and the heavens rejoice, when upon the altar the Son of the living God is in the hands of the priest!"

The life and love of Saint Francis, who modeled Christ in his life, his preaching, his very flesh, seems to be a thing of legend, but his life is very real. His sermons were short and simple and were reflected in how he lived. Life in Christ is not complicated if we keep our focus solely on Him who will provide everything for us if we but trust Him. That does not mean there will not be troubles or obstacles, but a life in Christ with the promise of heaven is worth giving up everything for. Some are called to trust in God in answering a call to the priesthood or religious life. Like the Poverello of Assisi, to hear God's voice and trust in Him, we must Be Still ... Be Not Afraid, to What is Jesus Calling You?

* * *

There is so much more to the life of Saint Francis than can be expressed in just a few pages. For Saint Francis, his love of God was so overwhelming that nothing else mattered. To lose that love of God was to lose one's soul. For Saint Francis, the thought of even a single soul separated from God was true sorrow, for that was everlasting death. So Saint Francis would let nothing, no object, no person, no power separate him from God or become an object of the slightest concern. God would and did provide all that he ever needed.

It seems strange to us in this day of instant gratification, with everything needing to work faster, smarter, cooler, for someone to give up everything. For Saint Francis, however, he gained everything by accepting the only thing worth hanging onto, the love of God and His only Son, Jesus Christ. His iPod was the song of the birds; his photo album was the mountains, fields, and streams; his Facebook page was the interaction with people of high and low estate he met as he went where God called him to go. Saint Francis missed nothing, wanted for nothing, for he gained everything when he gave away all he had.

This contradiction is what Jesus' life, death, and resurrection is all about. We must die to self to find life in Jesus. Saint Francis understood that it is in giving that we receive, it is in forgiving that we are forgiven. We are not judged on what we have, but on what we give. There is a reason the life of Saint Francis still mesmerizes the soul, it is because we see Christ in Him. There was nothing else in Saint Francis's life to hide the presence of Jesus, which helps explain why so many of his time would choose to follow him in what was clearly a hard way of living.

Saint Francis said that we are to preach the Gospel always, and if necessary, to use words. His life was the Gospel message. Finding that one thing in life that will bring true happiness is not like searching for a needle in a haystack, for the only thing that can bring true happiness, true joy is Christ and He stands before us calling us by name to follow Him. Saint Francis got the message and realized that for him to follow the Lord, he could not be hauling around all of the baggage life can place on our shoulders. Our cross goes on our shoulders, not the worries and stuff of life. So while we are not all called to abandon all the comforts of life, we are called to make sure that we do not lose sight of the only thing that has value, Jesus.

Chapter 22

THE SAINTS FOLLOWED God wherever He led them. They had to be willing to go anywhere God wanted them and take on any task, no matter how daunting. Still, God never asked more of the saint than he or she was able to do with the gifts God poured out on them. Mother Cabrini, the first United States citizen to be named a saint, was the same way. She had plans for travel, but was directed to locations she did not originally want to go. Still, she embraced God's call and took His message with her everywhere she went. She refused to take "No" for an answer, knowing that regardless of the obstacles or the odds, if it was God's will, then it would be done. She overcame all doubts, all fears, all challenges to spread the Gospel throughout the Americas. She epitomizes what the Gospel tells us: If we seek, we will find, ask, and it shall be done for us, knock, and the door will be opened unto us.

SAINT FRANCESCA XAVIER CABRINI
(May 2011)

Obedience and perseverance are two qualities of the saints. Both require humility and faithfulness to God's call. They require trust that the path we follow is God's plan for us, even if it is not the path we wanted. For Francesca Cabrini, she dreamed of being a missionary to the Far East. While the Lord did not fulfill her dreams just as she had hoped, her obedience to His will and perseverance in the face of obstacles brought faith and hope to the Americas and a place in heaven for Francesca, the first United States citizen to be named a saint.

The golden haired, green-eyed Francesca was the youngest of 13 children born to Augustine and Stella Cabrini in a little village on the plains of Lombardy, Italy. Nine of their children had already passed away before reaching the age of 13. Francesca's sisters Rosa and Maddalena, the latter who had polio, and her young brother Giovanni awaited her in life. Because they feared Francesca would not last the night, she was baptized the day she was born, July 15, 1850.

Her father worked the farm and was known around town as the Christian Tower. The family would often gather around while he read to them from the Annals of the Propagation of the Faith. Francesca was taken with stories of missionary saints and loved to hear missionary priests and sisters talk of their work when they visited her church of Sant'Angelo. She too wanted to be a missionary, and for her, the destination would be China. While her sister scoffed at the idea, believing Francesca too weak for such work, her mother was more supportive, saying, "Francesca shall become whatever the Lord wills."

Francesca studied hard, even when her poor health kept her out of school. Rosa saw to it since she was also the local school teacher. Francesca also learned the duties of working the farm, tending the garden, helping in the vineyard, making butter and cheese, and all domestic chores, such as cleaning, cooking, sewing, and caring for the sick, all skills that would serve her well in her later vocation.

In 1859, war came to Lombardy, and the Cabrini house was overrun with soldiers. Most of the families in the village had fled, but the Cabrinis remained. Her father's faith and courage in the face of warring factions left an impression on the young Francesca.

At 18 years of age, Francesca applied to become a Daughter of the Sacred Heart. The mother superior denied her request, believing Francesca's health was too fragile to meet the demands of religious life. While saddened by her rejection, Francesca was all the more determined to fulfill her vocational call to become a missionary.

Francesca's father, mother, and sister Maddalena died the following year, 1869. She remained to work the farm with Rosa and Giovanni, while every evening for a year she cared for a poor mute covered in sores, who lived in a hovel not far down the road. Caring for the sick and outcast would also become a part of her future calling. Indeed, in 1872, when the region was overrun by smallpox, she cared for as many as she could until coming down with the disease herself. Rosa then held a perpetual vigil at her bedside until she recovered, a cure Francesca attributes to the Sacred Heart.

Upon her recovery, Francesca traveled to Vidordo at the request of the local priest to fill in for the school teacher who had fallen ill. The students were foul tempered and challenged her at every move while subjecting her to pranks of all sorts. Still, she provided a steady support and discipline in the classroom while praying constantly for her students. Over time, they were won over, realizing that she truly did love them. Francesca also applied to two religious orders seeking to become a sister, but was again rejected by both.

Her next assignment would be the springboard to her life's vocation. Her local priest was made a monsignor and moved to Codogno, not far up the road. There was an orphanage that needed to be reorganized. The two women who ran it had been stealing from the orphanage's funds and were abusive to the girls, but no one, not even the bishop, could contain them and they owned the only building where the church could house the orphanage. This request to help out for a few weeks was to last six grueling years.

Francesca was not welcomed upon her arrival on August 12, 1874, and was told, point blank, that she was not wanted. The girls, however, craved someone to care for them and they took to Francesca almost immediately. Francesca returned the daily abuse she received with kindness, while she worried terribly for the girls whose basic needs were not being met. So, she sent for soaps and linens, and other items they would need. She scrubbed the girls and she cleaned the orphanage, much to the outrage of her hosts.

Three years later, seven girls came to her wanting to become missionaries alongside her. She approached the local priest who approved her request. On September 14, 1877, Francesca and her first seven daughters made their vows. They would be tested by three more years of abuse at the House of Provenance before, at the encouragement of the local priest, she left to start her own order for missionary sisters, the Missionary Sisters of the Sacred Heart.

In doing so, she could not leave the orphans behind. She found a home that was in desperate need of repair, but marched out with the girls to their new home. Francesca was 30 years old. She and the girls had to master carpentry, bricklaying, cleaning, painting, and all other sorts of crafts to get the house in order. They worked side by side with the work crews and by themselves into the night to save on money and prepare their home and school. It was a ritual she would perform dozens of times over the years.

By 1887, Francesca had started seven houses in the area. She was now growing impatient to begin her missionary work. She was, after all, now 37-years-old. So, she told her priest that she was going to Rome to seek permission to begin her work as a missionary. Even his skepticism and suggestion that she be satisfied with the work she was doing locally did not dampen her determination. With barely enough for the train fare, she and another sister headed to Rome.

Francesca spent her first three days trying to get an appointment with Cardinal Parocchi who could assist her in her quest. A home in Rome was needed to position her order for missionary work. At first, he listened with admiration, but in the end told her that her order was too young, too small, and did not have the resources for such an endeavor. While devastated, Francesca did not give up. She returned again and again to soften his heart to her request. Then, on October 22nd, the Cardinal said he had a request. He asked her to found not one but two houses in Rome, one a free school and the other a nursery. He would equip the school, but the sisters would have to provide for themselves, including finding a way to pay the rent.

Overjoyed, Francesca set right to work. Several sisters from Codogno joined in the effort and soon both houses were up and running. She received her official recognition as an institute on March 12, 1888.

Bishop Giovanni Scalabrini had great passion for the welfare of emigrants. Given the political and economic times, he helped many Italians leave their homeland to find work to provide for their families. Still, he worried for their spiritual well-being. So, he approached Francesca about taking her missionaries to America rather than China. She listened, but was not convinced.

In early 1889, Francesca was to have her first meeting with Pope Leo XIII. That very morning, Bishop Scalabrini told her that the Archbishop of New York had an orphanage for her if she would come to America. He had the letter of request with him, which he presented to Francesca. She was filled with fear and trepidation and did not know why. When she went to see Pope Leo, who would be of great spiritual comfort to Francesca over the next several decades, she presented herself to him for his blessing. Pope Leo was gravely concerned about the rise of materialism and the exploitation of the worker. After a brief discussion of her family, her childhood, and her order, he commented, "Sweet Daughter, Cardinal Parocchi and other of my good sons tell me you dream of bearing the light to the Orient." Then, regarding her thoughtfully, he said, "No, the house and family of western civilization must first be put in order. His love must conquer the West before we approach the East. There are sad truths you will learn by seeing with your own eyes. America, growing in titanic strides, will soon achieve world influence. If she becomes another soulless Babylon, she will topple, and with her fall she will drag down lesser nations, and the Christian labors for centuries." He concluded, "I desire very much a great missionary expansion in America. Francesca Cabrini, go to America. Plant there, and cultivate the beautiful fruit of Christ." On March 23, 1889, Francesca and six daughters sailed for New York.

Francesca and her sisters arrived at Ellis Island on March 31, 1889. No one was there to meet them. They found their way to San Gioacchino's church, a local parish for Italian immigrants. The priests were hospitable, but very poor. They arranged a room for them for the night at a local place, but it was a house of horrors with bugs and rats running amok. When Francesca was able to meet with the archbishop, she learned there was no orphanage and his letter asking her to delay her trip had never arrived. He told her he was sorry, but that she should return to Italy. In her typical fashion she told him that the Lord called her here, the Pope sent her here, and here was where she was going to stay. Impressed, he suggested she start with a small school at San Gioacchino's.

In her typical fashion, she got right to work. Soon, 200 children were enrolled and many adults sought her out for religious education. She saw the dire need of the immigrants who were desperately poor in materials and spirit. They were outcasts and taken advantage of at every turn, whether in work, housing, or medical care. This was why she had come to America.

Mother Cabrini met with the donor of the original five thousand dollars for the orphanage. She looked at the place where the woman wanted the orphanage and felt it would work. The bishop disagreed, but given Francesca's determination, let them raise the money they needed. Again, with their own labor and solicitation of things they needed such as beds, food, clothing, and basic necessities, they opened their orphanage. The local community, poor as it was, gave whatever she and the girls needed. She found orphan girls living in abandoned rooms and running the streets. She provided them with love and a safe place to live. They returned her kindness and became models of Christ's love.

Soon, they were out of space. They needed a place where the girls could run free. The Franciscans had a large house on a large piece of property by the river, and in her typical fashion, she worked a deal with the Franciscans to obtain the home for her orphanage. This she would do often in her ministry by appealing to people's hearts for her orphans.

Francesca did not stop at the needs of her orphans. She opened Columbus Hospital in New York as a place for immigrants to receive quality health care. Again, the outpouring of support was in answer to her prayers. While she had nothing but her soul to offer, the Lord provided as He said He always would. Within six years, the hospital was expanded to 100 beds and was the most modern of New York hospitals.

Mother Cabrini's efforts spread throughout the United States to Chicago, New Orleans, Denver, Los Angeles, and Seattle, among other places. It was in Seattle in 1903 that she walked into city hall and asked to become a United States citizen and that is what she was when she walked back out onto the streets of the city.

She opened schools, orphanages, and hospitals wherever they were needed. She obtained funds and support from the people who owned the property she wanted and those who had what she needed. She faced hostile governments in Panama, survived malaria in Argentina, and opened homes throughout Central and South America, not to mention Europe. By 1914, Mother Cabrini had opened 65 houses around the Americas and Europe, drawing in 1500 sisters, and helping countless orphans, students, and patients. She died in Chicago on December 22, 1917, while being cared for in the hospital she founded. At her request, she was buried in New York.

Mother Cabrini embraced America, knowing as Pope Leo XIII did that to be a shining city on a hill, the light of the people must be the Light of the World, Jesus Christ. With material opportunity in abundance, the grace of God must be there, as well. She brought that to the poor, the sick, the suffering, the abandoned. She did so in the face of every obstacle, knowing that the Lord would always provide, and He did.

We must have such obedience and perseverance. The devil will try to trip us up, but the obstacles and objections we face doing God's will are mere tests of our faithfulness. If we remain faithful, all things are possible. Our adventure in life with Christ will be remarkable if we follow the path He sets out for us. As a religious, Mother Cabrini was devoted entirely to Christ, and through her His light shined throughout our land. What is our path? To discover it, Be Still … Be Not Afraid, To What is Jesus Calling You?

* * *

"No trial has come to you but what is human. God is faithful and will not let you be tried beyond your strength; but with the trial he will also provide a way out, so that you may be able to bear it." (1 Cor. 10:13) This reminder from Saint Paul exemplifies Saint Cabrini. She overcame every obstacle that was thrown in her path. She defeated her own physical weakness, she defied expectations and did what many thought was impossible when it came to establishing homes and schools for orphans and hospitals for those who most needed quality and compassionate health care. Those who would have never dreamed of coming to the aid of this or any poor nun did so with gracious hearts after meeting her. The reason is simple, Christ traveled with Mother Cabrini, who placed her complete and total trust in the Lord to accomplish the good she was convinced she was called to do in His name.

Mother Cabrini was told many times that she was too weak to be a missionary, yet she traveled the western world, over mountains and across oceans to spread God's love to people yearning for their God. She was committed to doing God's work and nothing was going to stand in her way. No matter the trial, God gave her the means to bear it and accomplish what He set out for her to do. She knew when to persevere and when to brush the dust from her feet as condemnation of those towns and people who would not accept God's love. She was the face of Jesus to everyone she met and no matter the conditions, she found a way to remain focused on the only thing that mattered, doing God's will for His glory.

We can learn much from Mother Cabrini. God is calling us to help build His kingdom. There are many tasks to be done in this endeavor and we will only be asked to do those things God is prepared to help us achieve. Our focus need only be on Him and realize that no calling is too big or too small if done for the glory and love of God. Life will throw obstacles in our way, but if we remain focused and determined, we will overcome any obstacle and pass every test for God will be with us.

Evil is real and Satan cannot bear to see the love of Jesus spread in our world. He will do everything in his power to stop the work of those who profess Jesus as Lord from doing God's will. As Jesus told us in the beatitudes, "Blessed are they who are persecuted for the sake of righteousness, for theirs is the kingdom of heaven." (Matthew 5:10) Trust in the Lord in those times and know that He is with you. If it be His will, you will accomplish what is before you. Keep the faith and persevere. Do not lose hope. God is calling you for something great, for all things that further the kingdom of God are indeed great. Mother Cabrini accomplished so much with so little because she relied totally on God, and He remained true to His word that He would provide. The same promise is made to us if we just trust Him.

Chapter 23

ALL OF THE saints had an intimate connection with Jesus. The life of Jesus began with Mary saying "yes" to God's call. His entrance into the world was in the quiet of a stable. The angels proclaimed His birth, the shepherds came to pay Him homage, men from the East traveled long and far to bring Him gifts fit for a king. Each of the saints also proclaimed His birth, paid Him homage, and traveled long and far to bring Him gifts fit for the King of Kings. They proclaimed that the Lord was real and that His love was real. They praised Him with their lives, and some with their deaths. They gave Him all they had, their very lives, which is just what the king wanted. Our gift to the Lord is not our belongings, but our very selves. When we give that gift, as the saints did, we sing a song as powerful and beautiful as the choir of angels that first Christmas night. We then proceed to "Go, Tell it on the Mountain" that Jesus Christ was born. Our lives are a testament to that great gift from God, His only begotten Son, Jesus.

We each have our own traditions to celebrate the birth of Jesus. The same is true for the saints. What follows is just a small reflection on how a few saints either celebrated Christmas or influenced how we celebrate the great feast of our Savior's birth today.

CHRISTMAS 2010

The Third Sunday of Advent is called Gaudete Sunday, which means "rejoice." As Saint Paul said, "Rejoice in the Lord always, again, I say Rejoice." Our time of waiting is almost over and we should rejoice in the birth of our Savior.

In considering our reflection for Christmas, I reflected on the lives of the nearly 20 saints we have talked about from 2006 to 2010. Each of them lived lives very different from each other in walking the roads the Lord asked them to follow. But each shared the same faith in Christ, the child born that day in Bethlehem two thousand years ago. The story of their lives, each and every one of them, is to rejoice in the Lord, to rejoice always in all circumstances in the Lord. That theme was evident in the stories we considered for each saint, whether it was Saints Peter and Paul, Saint Francis and Saint Catherine of Siena, or Saint Padre Pio and Mother Teresa. They all rejoiced in the Lord and bore their sufferings with joy, for they carried their crosses for Jesus.

Christmas 2009 we had a parish Advent retreat. The two nights had as their themes "The Gift" of Christmas and "The Song" of Christmas. The Gift of Christmas centered on the story of Maria, a poor girl who found a dirt-covered bird with a broken wing. She spent the little money she had on a cage made of sticks and twine, collected corn that had dropped on the ground, and cared for the humble looking creature. When Christmas came, Maria went to the church on Christmas Eve with her small bird in its ragged cage.

As Maria entered the church, she saw the nativity set with all sorts of lavishly wrapped gifts, which had been left in celebration of Jesus' birth. She waited in the back until the service was over before approaching to see the wonder of the scene. In the stillness of the church, Maria was self conscious that her meager gift was unworthy of the King of Kings. Then, in the silence she heard a voice that said, "Maria, what brings you to me? If the bird in the cage is your offering, open the door and let me see." When she did, the bird flew out and soared to the rafters.

As the bells tolled the arrival of Christmas, the bird began to sing. It was the most beautiful of songs, and it filled the church. Maria's heart was filled with joy. The song of the Nightingale was not only the most beautiful she had ever heard, but it also announced to all who could hear that Jesus Christ had been born. Maria's gift was everything she had, which made it more precious than all of the beautifully wrapped gifts that surrounded the nativity scene. You see, what Maria offered the Lord when she opened the cage and let the bird fly out was herself.

From the Nightingale's song, we learned what "The Song of Christmas" was all about. First, each of us has our own song, but the purpose of the song is the same. It is the same as the Nightingale's song. It ushers in Christmas, a time of rejoicing in Jesus our Lord. Our song during that night of the retreat was "Go Tell It on the Mountain." Our lives are to be a song that proclaims that Jesus Christ is Born, that God loves us so much that He sent His only Son into the world to save us from sin. Our lives are our song of Christmas. The question is: What do our lives proclaim?

For the saints, their gift to the Lord was their very lives, all that they had and all they would become. They followed the Lord on the path He set out before them. In doing so, they sang of the Lord's goodness announcing to all, from Popes and Kings to sinners and outcasts that Jesus Christ is Born.

Three of our saints had particular incidents in their lives that have a specific connection to Christmas. The first was Saint Therese of Lisieux. As she grew up, her family tradition was to leave shoes in the fireplace. The family would go to Midnight Mass and upon returning home, she would put her coat and hat away and rush back down stairs to open the gifts that filled her shoes. When she was little, this tradition brought great joy to her father who loved watching his youngest show such delight in the magic of the presents in her shoes. As she grew older, this tradition proved to be important in her maturity that formed the foundation of her vocation.

On Christmas 1886, when she was 13-years-old and already set on following her older sister to the convent, Therese came home from Midnight Mass again excited about the presents in her shoes. When her father noticed her shoes positioned in the fireplace, he became uncharacteristically upset and commented that he was glad it was the last year the family needed to keep the tradition. Therese did not hear him, but her sister Celine did. Celine went upstairs to encourage Therese to not go back downstairs. She told her, "Taking the presents out of your shoes will upset you too much." Therese understood, but went down anyway. Normally, such a situation would have caused Therese to break down in tears, but this night she says the Lord returned to her a strength of soul she had not had since her mother died almost ten years earlier. She opened her gifts with such incredible joy that everyone was extremely happy. Saint Therese says that night, as they celebrated the birth of Jesus, she moved from any thoughts of selfishness to pure happiness. She showed this happiness in all she did and with all she met until the day she died on September 30, 1897.

Saint Therese's family tradition can be traced back to one of the Church's earliest saints, Saint Nicholas. While his generosity was not tied directly to the celebration of Christmas, it has come to define our celebration of the Lord's birth. You may recall that a local man had three daughters, but no money for a dowry. When he was out of money and on the verge of having to send his oldest daughter to a brothel, the kindly Bishop of Myra went by the house in the quiet of night and tossed a bag of gold through the open window. The gold was enough to pay a dowry and provide for the family for a year. This happened two more times with Saint Nicholas coming through each time the man was in desperate straits and needed a miracle to provide for his family.

Saint Nicholas gave from his own funds in the quiet of the night to serve Jesus by helping someone in need. He did so not for the glory that would come to him from being generous, but to complete the work the Lord called each of His disciples to fulfill, to love their neighbor. We do the same thing when we participate in the Giving Tree at Saint Matthew's or the many random acts of kindness we do this time of year.

Of course, our vision of Christmas centers on the stable where Jesus was born. He is seen lying on the hay in the manger surrounded by Mary, Joseph and a few animals. The shepherds then appear after hearing the angels announce the Birth of the Savior. That vision comes to us as much from Saint Luke's description in his gospel as it does from Saint Francis's celebration of Christmas in 1223.

Saint Francis loved Christmas. He was always so moved by the humility and poverty of the Lord's birth and the sacrifice of the Blessed Mother. He wanted to do something special for Christmas so he could experience more fully the joy of Christmas and the holy poverty our Lord welcomed with his humble beginning. So, when leaving Rome for the last time, he told Pope Honorius what he wanted to do, and the Pope granted his permission.

Saint Francis was friends with the lord of Greccio who had entered the Order of Penance. Next to Greccio was a hillside honeycombed with caves and upon which was a small woods. Saint Francis told him that he wanted to experience the Lord's birth in Bethlehem by setting up a real manger with hay and bringing in an ox and an ass that had been present to keep the Christ Child warm that first Christmas night. The man was only too delighted to help.

That night, the town's people and the Franciscans gathered round on the hillside with torches, which illuminated the scene much like the star that shined so brightly at the Lord's birth. A procession made its way up the hill to the manger where Saint Francis stood, deeply moved at the sight.

They celebrated Mass on a niche just above the spot where the Crib was set up. Saint Francis served as a deacon at the Mass, read the Gospel and gave one of his more moving homilies. The celebrant at Mass confessed that he had never experienced such consolation while celebrating the divine mysteries.

That night of the living nativity was like no other night. Several later claimed to have seen the Christ Child appear in the manger as if asleep, except for the moment when He opened His eyes and smiled at Saint Francis. Not since the shepherds arrived at the stable in Bethlehem had people experienced the Birth of the Lord with such awe, such joy. Indeed, it could be said that we have living nativity celebrations today because of Saint Francis.

Christmas is a time of rejoicing, a time of happiness and good cheer. The stress of shopping, attending parties, and making sure we check our lists twice can take our focus off the true gift of Christmas and silence our song. At Christmastime, take the time to rejoice in the Birth of the Lord. Let your words and actions announce from the mountaintop that Jesus

Christ is born. The lives of the saints sang out that good news everyday. We are called to do the same. When we do, we will find true joy, true peace, true happiness. Merry Christmas.

* * *

The celebration of Christmas is the celebration of the birth of a savior. Saint Francis was moved to recount the birth of Christ. Saint Nicholas was moved to live his life being generous to those in need and speaking boldly the truths of our faith. Saint Therese learned that you enjoy Christmas with a childlike wonderment, but you do not get obsessed with the wrappings, but with the true treasure that is Jesus.

We decorate our homes and put on our finest clothes. That is as it should be for we are truly preparing to welcome the Christ Child into our homes and into our lives. You would clean and make everything look its best when expecting company, so how much more do we do when we are preparing to welcome Jesus at Christmas. The hope is that as we put up the tree, the garland, the lights, the stockings, we remember to stand in wonder as the shepherds did and to prepare our gifts for the Lord as the Magi did. In our family, we find a place of prominence for our Nativity scene. My kids help in picking out gifts for people based on tags from the giving tree at church. They have learned that Christmas is not just the time to receive but to be generous, generous with our time, our talent, and our treasure.

The shepherds and the Magi came and worshiped, but then had to go home. The Christmas season ends and rolls into January. While we do not hear anything more of the shepherds or Magi in the Gospels, we can only imagine that the experience of Christ's birth had a profound impact on at least some of them. So it should for us as we contemplate how we are called to serve Christ.

God withheld nothing from us when He sent His only Son into the world. Jesus was born into poverty, vulnerable, but not alone. Every child, whether born into want or plenty, has the ability and potential to change the world by carrying on the mission of the Child born in a stable, wrapped in swaddling clothes and found lying in a manger. How we live, in our families, in our work, and in our communities, should announce that Jesus Christ is born.

When the tree is taken down and all the wrapping paper and boxes and bows have found their way out, the Child remains. Do we really rejoice in His birth and in His life, death and resurrection? Do we reflect the simplicity of that scene in our interaction with others? Are we guided by that star of faith that may lead us to places we never imagined to take our gifts and talents to use in glorifying God? The journey may be across the street to a neighbor, or, as with some of the saints, halfway around the world to a foreign land. The journey may take us into the slums or into the palaces of the world, always with the purpose of taking the Gospel with us. "For a child will lead them," and that child is Jesus Christ. We have to make sure He is the one that leads us.

Chapter 24

FROM THE BEGINNING of human history, God has revealed Himself to man for the purpose of letting us know He loves us and that He is calling us to something incredible. God does not force His love on us, for you cannot make someone love you, but He calls us to love. With sin, we are separated from God, which means there needs to be reconciliation to reunite that which was broken. Jesus came to reconcile us with the Father and did so by shedding His blood on the cross. Our path to God, therefore, includes the cross.

With the cross before us, we have a clear path to follow. Given that path, too many are afraid to follow, choosing instead to accept what they know, what appears to be easier, and forgoing the good that awaits. So, to help guide us and to remind us of God's love, the Lord sent prophets to prepare us for the coming of Christ and He has sent His saints to show us what it means to follow Jesus.

In reading Scripture, it is easy to say, "I know what it says, but what does it mean for me?" God's Truth is the same today as it was when the world began and it will be the same when the world passes away. The saints, people just like all of us, with their own faults and eccentricities, overcame everything to discover what Jesus was calling them to do. They set aside personal desire and picked up their cross. They came to realize that the only way to be free was to obey God's commands, for it is outside of God's commands that we encounter the bonds of sin and death. The "rules" were not chains to hold us down, but guideposts to keep us safe.

The saints took the Lord's words found in the seventh chapter of Matthew's Gospel to heart, where it is written: "Jesus said to his disciples: 'Not everyone who says to me, 'Lord, Lord,' will enter the Kingdom of heaven, but only the one who does the will of my Father in heaven. … Everyone who listens to these words of mine and acts on them will be like a wise man who built his house on rock. The rain fell, the floods came, and the winds blew and buffeted the house. But it did not collapse; it had been set solidly on rock. And everyone who listens to these words of mine, but does not act on them, will be like a fool who built his house on sand. The rain fell, the floods came and the winds blew and buffeted the house. And it collapsed and was completely ruined.'"

Saints built their lives on the rock of faith, on Jesus who is the same Yesterday, Today, and Forever. Their lives were not founded on the latest fad or the philosophy of the day that would change tomorrow. To do so would be like betting your life on the stock market and hoping you picked the right stock as the foundation for all you did and believed. It may have been a great pick when you selected it, but when times or circumstances change, it has no substance to help it last, so it collapses.

Faith is not a "get with the times" to be modified and tinkered with to fit the now of today. God's Truth is timeless and the lessons of Scripture are as true today as when they were written and Jesus' words carry the same importance as the day they were uttered. That means the Biblical truths of right and wrong still apply and the saints lived by that ever constant, ever stable, ever strong faith. No wonder they could overcome every obstacle and withstand every storm.

There is a reason that when Jesus founded the Church, He did so on "the Rock" of Peter. Not just on the man, but on the faith as Peter expressed it, that Jesus is the Son of the Living God. It was to Peter that Christ gave the keys to the Kingdom of God and the authority to declare what was good and acceptable and what was improper and forbidden. (Matthew 16:16-19.) Jesus promised that the Church would be guided by the Holy Spirit who is "the Spirit of truth" and who "will guide you to all truth." (John 16:5-15.) And so the Church leads us in the truth that is Jesus, always pointing us to Him. The saints understood this, so they prayed for the Church and lived as integral members of the Church.

When Peter began to sink after stepping out of the boat in the storm to walk on the water toward Jesus, he did so because he took his eye off the One who has dominion over the storm and over the sea. The lives of the saints teach us that we are to keep our eye focused squarely on Jesus and to live according to His teachings. If we do, we may be chastised or called out of touch, but we will be living in the Truth. If we do, we will never be disappointed. With all of the challenges the saints faced, they were never disappointed in the path God laid out before them.

In following Him, Jesus did not ask us to go it alone, but called us to community. So, we learn from each other as members of His Church. We gather in prayer groups because we learn so much from the faith experiences of others and by sharing our own faith experiences. We come together to worship the Lord as a family. That does not mean there are not times when we need to be alone with the Lord. On the contrary, there are many such times, but that does not take away from what we learn from our brothers and sisters and from being a part of Christ's Church.

The saints are our brothers and sisters in faith, and their lives are the best examples we have of what it means to be a follower of Jesus. We should take the time to learn about them and to learn from them. Indeed, so many of the saints learned from the saints who came before them and found in their lives great examples to follow. We pray to the saints for their guidance and encouragement as we walk along our faith journey. As with our friends and neighbors, it should be comforting to know that we can have the likes of Saint Francis or Saint Catherine or Saint Peter or Saint Paul walk with us; that we can benefit from the intercession of the Blessed Mother just as the newlyweds did at Cana. The reason is simple; we are all God's children. We all seek to obtain the Kingdom of God. There are so many people available to pray for us and with us, we should not forget those who have gone before us and have received the promise of eternal glory when looking for help and examples of how to deal with the pressures of everyday life. The saints experienced far greater worries than we will ever experience, and they conquered sin and death by faith in Jesus Christ.

God has a plan and a purpose for us all. That plan is a good one, filled with wonders and joys beyond our imagining. To experience what God has in store for us, we must only follow Him. That does not mean there will not be obstacles in our way or bends in the road that make us want to turn back, but we walk with Christ so we have nothing to fear. God does not give us more than we can handle, but we have to carry our cross if we want to get through it. The saints learned that lesson. Some learned it early in life while others, like Saint Augustine, took a little longer to figure it out.

While everyone is not called to religious life, everyone is called to be a saint. Only saints are in heaven and that is the promise Jesus offers us if we follow Him. God calls us to Himself for the purpose of building His kingdom. How we answer that call is what life is all about. The promise of heaven that comes from living a life of faith in Jesus Christ is the pearl worth discovering and the field worth buying. It is worth giving up everything to obtain. It will take dedication and courage on our part, but with faith the size of a mustard seed, we will succeed.

So, in closing, I want to leave you with a prayer attributed to Thomas Merton, a twenty century Trappist monk who lived in the Abbey of Gethsemani, Kentucky, and died in 1968. His journey to faith is recounted in his autobiography, *The Seven Storey Mountain.* When it comes to following the path God lays out for us, I have found comfort in these words:

> *My Lord God, I have no idea where I am going. I do not see the road ahead of me. I cannot know for certain where it will end. Nor do I really know myself, and the fact that I think that I am following your will does not mean that I am actually doing so. But I believe that the desire to please you does in fact please you. And I hope I have that desire in all that I am doing. I hope that I will never do anything apart from that desire. And I know that if I do this you will lead me by the right road, though I may know nothing about it. Therefore will I trust you always, though I may seem to be lost and in the shadow of death. I will not fear, for you are ever with me, and you will never leave me to face my perils alone.*

To answer God's call takes a leap of faith and it takes an effort to know the Scriptures and the teachings of the Church. It takes time spent in prayer and learning from those who went before us who walked with the Lord. It takes a life built on the rock of faith, the truth that is Jesus Christ.

But even with the uncertainty of Thomas Merton's words and the fact we do not get angels to speak to us in dreams to tell us what our next step in life is supposed to be, God's plan for you is knowable. His truth is not a mystery to be decoded or subject to varying and contradictory interpretations. He founded the Church to protect and teach the faith, so we have Christ's teaching as handed down to us from the apostles and their successors. We have the Scriptures that lay out the beautiful story of salvation. Christ has given us everything we need and He is calling us.

The time to hear God's voice is now. The time to live a life proud of the Gospel is now. The time to serve God as He is calling us to serve Him is now. So, Be Still … Be Not Afraid. To What is Jesus Calling You?

Made in the USA
Charleston, SC
04 July 2015